COMPELLED BY
GRACE

ROCKYFLEMING //

Compelled by Grace
Copyright © 2010 by Rocky Fleming
Published by Prayer Cottage Publications
P.O. Box 5097
Bella Vista, AR 72714

www.influencers.org

ISBN 978-1-936417-01-8

"From the fullness of his grace we have all received one blessing after another."
— John 1:16 NIV

CONTENTS

INTRODUCTION

As a writer, I believe that I have been given a unique benefit having been raised in Mississippi by Southern parents along with my extended family of grandparents, aunts, uncles and their friends. They were people who lived in a rural area far away from big cities. They were strong people who had weathered the Great Depression and many other challenges that threatened their survival. They were good people whose faith had been rooted in God's Holy Word, and it was firmly established in their lives because of their hard circumstances. Their difficult lives also made it easy to recognize how desperate they would be without Christ. As a result, they were people who were forged by God into godly men and women.

But, they would also be described by most people as "common, ordinary and insignificant," for that is the world's view of such people. Today, they would be dismissed as irrelevant by the high-powered chargers of our society, and they would not be listened to. Even in their own time period they were disregarded by the wealthy and "important," for they lived simple, uncomplicated lives in the country. They didn't have a great deal of formal education, and certainly very little in the way of material comforts. But to me, they were pioneers, saints and heroes, providing the very foundation of my faith.

These people were also wonderful storytellers, and the wisdom they shared with me still influences me to this day. In my early childhood days, we were without television. Therefore, since they perfected the art of spinning a tale, my listening to their stories became my greatest form of entertainment.

As a writer, it has also become a storehouse of human-interest stories, sage advice and word pictures that make me "see" things and try to describe them in my writing. Little wonder when I write a book and attempt to convey God's wisdom and intimacy with Him, I tend to travel back in time and to a place where I once sat at the feet of these wonderful saints.

Sure, I had my own time of rebellion in my teenage years, when trying to look through the eyes of these older people became a challenge to me. But, as I have grown older, I have begun to cherish the earthy wisdom of these country folks, and see life differently. I see in their wisdom an uncluttered simplicity that helps me sift through the complexities of this day and time, and to find satisfying answers quickly.

I have come to realize that they had life figured out in many ways better than the theories espoused by those experts who tell us how to live a successful life. But, their package was so simple and plain that most people were unwilling to unwrap it and look at the treasure it contained. However, as I've grown older, I have begun to reopen this package God gave to me, and look more closely at the wisdom they shared to a child who sat at their feet. What I have been rediscovering is making a lot of sense.

In my previous book, *The Journey to the Inner Chamber*, which is an allegory, I introduced fictional characters and events to the reader in order to convey deeper truths about an intimate, abiding relationship with Christ. I say they are "fictional," but in fact they are real to me, for I drew them from memories of people I have known and loved, as well from my own personal experiences. Although I gave them different names and placed them in a different setting from the real persons, the characters represented the life of a person I have known, or have known about.

Some people have asked me if the characters in the book are real. When they find out they are not, they are often disappointed, because they seem so real. There is a reason that the characters seem so alive, for they are real to me. They only have different names and live in a different place from the real people I used to model them after. Gabe is one of those characters, and is especially loved by readers. He deeply encourages us, for in him we see true, godly influence at work.

Actually, "Gabe" is a metaphor for a man or woman who truly walks with Christ. He is everything we want to be as a Christian, for he has found contentment, joy and great purpose. These are things most people want, but are not able to find. Gabe is a man who needs no applause from mankind, for he enjoys it from his walk with Christ. Gabe is courageous, he is influential and he is a man with purpose. But, he is not defined by his wealth or lack of it. He is not limited because of his circumstances, and he has nothing to prove in order to win approval. He already has approval from the King of Kings.

When we study Gabe, we are encouraged, for we understand that we can all be like him and embrace those same traits. With Gabe, we can see a path that if we follow, we can encounter the same God he serves and enjoy the same fellowship with Him that Gabe has. Looking at Gabe encourages us to know that this kind of fellowship with Christ, and this kind of demeanor that grows from it, are available for all God's children.

Because of the great response to Gabe, and the insights many people have learned from him, I have been urged to write again, and to bring more people like him to light. Therefore, this book has been written so that we can continue to hear wisdom from people like Gabe, and to understand better what it means to walk with Christ. If you ask me, as others have before, I will tell you that the people you will read about in this book are fictional characters. But, in my heart I know they are real. I still hear their voices and follow their wisdom as they call out to me from the front porch of a simple house in Mississippi and invite me to "Come and sit awhile, 'cause I have something to tell you."

It has been over 50 years since I sat at their feet, but the insight they gave me, and the life they modeled before me, stays with me until this day. Am I wrong to answer as I did that the characters in this book are not real? Maybe I should answer simply, "Yes, they are real, for I have known them."

I will leave that up to you to decide, after you read this book. You might also want to look around, for there might be a "Gabe" who has been living near you and you never realized it. Best of all, maybe there is a "Gabe" in you begging to come to life. Are you ready to let him come out?

I hope this book will encourage you to let him do so, for we need more men like him in this world.

— Rocky Fleming

CHAPTER ONE

Gabe's Valley

The last few yards to the scenic overlook of the valley are the hardest for me to get to now. I can't say it is because it is steeper and the path more rugged. No excuse to be found there. Rather, I have to make peace with reality and just accept the fact the rugged hikes I once could take without a stop for breath are fading as each year passes. It challenges my "mature" bones and muscles each time I do it. But the reward of seeing the valley is always worth my effort.

"Gabe's Valley" is the affectionate name I've given to the most precious piece of real estate I've ever seen. At its center is an 80-acre plot with a hundred year-old farmhouse and barn that occupies this particular piece of the valley. To me the farm is the heart of the valley, for the spiritual legacy that lingers in and around the old home place has been the epicenter of many blessings to the valley, and even to the world.

Oh yes, there is a lot of natural beauty to see, as a small stream begins high in the mountains and snakes it way though the valley, while touching all the farms it flows past. The water is crystal clear and fish abundant, for the stream serves as a natural watering system for the rich valley. Through years of floods and run offs, a heavy layer of dark topsoil has been deposited on the valley floor making the gardens and pastures grown in the fertile vale turn into a lush haven for vegetables and fruit. Everything, including the cattle and sheep, has a healthy look. Even the gravel road winding through the valley floor provides an abundance of wild berries in the summer of the year, as they cling to the fencing rails lining the road. All summer, wild flowers grow and fill in every open space not cultivated, providing a tapestry of variegated beauty throughout the valley.

When I scan the land below, my eyes feast and my soul is refreshed by the view. I bow my head in sincere worship and whisper a prayer:

> *"Father, what beauty You have created. Thank You for opening my eyes to see it and my heart to appreciate it. Thank You for inviting me to this place to spend time alone with You. I am overwhelmed by Your love and Your creation. May I never cease seeing, feeling and enjoying what You desire to bring me to when I am alone with You. Lord Jesus, take me deeper to the place where You and I can abide. I know there is still more to understand, and you want me to experience it in that precious place with You."*

As I lean back against a large boulder, I spend the rest of the afternoon in a surreal state that intertwines prayer and communion with God, while being totally immersed in my surroundings. Every bird catches my stare. There is a majestic bald eagle soaring eye level with me as it skims the ridge around the valley and rides a thermal across the valley below. I join with him in spirit as he has me with him in his dance with the thermals. I imagine seeing the valley through his eyes. He glides effortlessly over the deepest part of the valley, and when a slight updraft lifts one of his wings, he turns lazily into the updraft, and in an instant rises hundreds of feet, while riding the air current. I am in awe of my Savior's creation.

The clouds are intermittently causing the sun to cast shadows across the valley, while highlighting and concealing different areas on its floor. With each highlighted view, I am able to see and appreciate another aspect of the valley floor, almost as if a spotlight is focused on it. This evokes another prayer:

> *"Savior, life is like that, isn't it? We think we have something figured out completely only to have you shine Your light on it in such a way to make us see things differently and more clearly, and we wonder why we hadn't seen it this way before."*

With this last insight, my mind quickly travels back to the many things I now see differently. People, such as family, friends and enemies alike, are looked at differently now. I suppose you could say the light of grace given to me has opened my eyes to a different world and the people who live in it, as both beauty and corruption are equally revealed and understood. I have come to see that the inner qualities in all of God's creation have a unique beauty, and given the opportunity to escape the corruption the bondage of sin or wounds from others brings, are able to become a blessing to the beholder, and bring much glory to God.

I have been shown it is God's magnificent grace that enables us all to be transformed into something uniquely beautiful, as this part of us can be released from the crusted shell of our fallen nature and be free to express a new life.

But it does not come easily. With sober reality, I have seen there is a life-altering struggle required to find this freedom, and I personally know my new view has not come easily for me, or for the ones who have invested their lives in me, so that I could see things differently. I have come to see my life story is not mine alone, for it also very much the story of another man or woman's faith that has eventually born its fruit in me. Like their stories and the ways they have intermingled with mine, I have come to understand a life

11

story, good or bad, will live after us. As I think on this last insight, I ask,

"Father, what will my story be like in the end?"

I again look at the beautiful valley below and think, "With such abundance and tranquility, I would think any and everyone in such a place as this would be at peace with his or her own life and the neighbors who live next to each other." But, I know from its history, the legacy of faith that emerged within the confines of the valley and its hills had to be forged by threat of life, bigotry, hatred, forgiveness and restoration with the grace only God could provide.

Oh, there is now a spirit of peace flowing from the people who live in this valley. It is the Spirit of the Living God Who has made His way to the surface of our lives and we are able to see it, and find encouragement from it.

However, it was not always this way. In fact, there was a malevolent element hidden from sight, deep within the people, which would not allow harmony and peace to be found between one another. It was dark and insidious. It corrupted the very soul of the valley. This evil not only did its work in the people, as it reproduced from one person to the next, it also strangely corrupted the very land they tried to work. The land itself became as ugly and desolate as the souls of the people who lived in the valley, except for one person and his special piece of the valley.

It is hard to look out over the beautiful valley now and imagine seeing it all desolate and unproductive, while the little, 80-acre plot Gabe lived on, and I now own, was lush and productive. There must have been some interesting discussions among the valley residents about this phenomenon. As peaceful as the valley is at present, one would never realize there was a great, spiritual warfare going on during a time that had to be fought and won using the only weapons that can win such battles, which are courage, faith, prayer and God's deliverance.

When I come to this place and overlook the valley, I often close my eyes and see past events like snapshots. They reveal a legacy of faith and godly wisdom that has grown in the healthy soil repentance and restoration gave to the people of the valley. Interwoven in the fabric of this valley emerged some very special people who were used to nurture a spiritual climate that would eventually embrace the differences of each person and encourage men and women to become the champions that God wanted to make of them. God used a few people as His voice and hands to reach other people of the valley, and to encourage them into a life changing, spiritual journey with Christ.

Eventually, there arose other people who, with God's help, conquered the evil that lay below the surface. What came out of the battle were a people after God's own heart.

In my own life, I have discovered when I find myself brought into God's plan to be His instrument of love and healing for someone else, I find my life is blessed as well. I have come to understand the deep purpose hidden within every real believer's heart is to find a true heart connection with God.

When we come into this proximity with Him, and slow down long enough to experience a love that only He can give, it transforms us. This in turn gives us purpose, and our hidden life with Christ eventually breaks to the surface and redefines our view of the people in our world, and their view of us. This is what happened to the people who lived in the valley years ago, and what led to a movement of God that sustains even to this day.

While scanning the valley, my eyes start to grow heavy. This happens to me a lot lately, and it seems to be a way of life now. I make myself as comfortable as possible against the boulder, for I know what is coming next. In my drowsiness, and just before dropping off to sleep, past faces and stories of certain people who lived in the valley come to mind. Their stories, as mine, are unique, and yet, somehow, a common thread connects us.

As I shared time with these people, I was introduced to an earthy wisdom that has been forgotten or overlooked by the busy rat race life gives us now days. I have come to call these insights, *Kingdom Secrets*. These secrets opened my eyes to many mysteries of God I had not known before. I can remember in great detail how God reached through these people into my life, and a piece of a puzzle was fitted together and began to show a beautiful picture of the Body of Christ, as we needed one another in order to understand what God wanted to say to us.

As I think about this, I pray again:

> *"Father, never let me forget what You have done in my life. Let me never forget the people who allowed You to work through their lives and how Your love eventually came to me through them. And Lord, for those You have allowed me to serve, let the most dominant thought they have about me be that my life reminded them of You."*

While I watch the valley below, I fade into my afternoon nap. The remembrance of bygone years rewinds in my dreams as if I were watching a story and the people of the valley who formed its unique personality.

Like most good dream stories, it has a beginning, and this one starts when I literally "bought the farm" twenty years before today. That was the first day I returned to the home I had never lived in, and when the *Kingdom Secrets* began to be revealed to me. Let me share with you my story, as I remember it in my dream.

CHAPTER TWO

The Secret of *Divine Orchestration*

T he day after we had closed the paperwork purchasing Gabe's farm, I turned into the narrow, winding, gravel road leading to the farmhouse. A flood of memories rushed at me as I did so.

I remembered the first time I saw the old house and the critical situation I was in. My truck had just run off the road into a snow-covered ditch. It was almost dark and deathly cold. I was stranded in the rural, farmland valley, having barely made it out alive from the mountains after an ill-advised camping trip. The snowstorm had been building all day and it finally hit with its full fury. I had been fighting it for hours, as I drove down from the mountains. The hidden rut pulling my truck into the ditch delivered a knockout blow to my plans for getting home safely and on time.

It was in this dismal condition I saw the old farmhouse and the welcoming smoke from its chimney that assured me someone was home. The farmhouse was now looking more ragged and rundown than the first day I saw it. But, it still welcomed me.

I stopped my truck before going any further down Gabe's road, so I could linger in the nostalgia a while longer. The inactive farm had become sacred grounds to me for several years since meeting its owner years before. This man understood some secrets of the Kingdom of Heaven, and was willing to abundantly share them with me. I had read the *Kingdom Secret* phrase in the Bible before, as Jesus spoke it to His disciples. But, as we often do, I failed to connect words spoken 2,000 years ago to the present day. It was after Gabe had died, and after hearing many stories of the man's influence, that I saw clearly he was one of those saints God had entrusted *Kingdom Secrets* with.

I opened the door and stood beside my truck. I scanned the eighty acres of overgrown pastureland and the unpainted farmhouse and barn. I whispered to myself, "There will be a lot of work to do, but it will be worth the effort."

While I looked at the farmhouse, I thought of memories of the old black man standing on the front porch, welcoming me with a wave of his hand, and gleaming white teeth in his smile that could be spotted from the end of his road. The first time I saw him on that stormy night was after my wreck. It was like a lifeline being thrown to a drowning person.

Gabe didn't know who I was, or if a dangerous person was knocking on his door. It was dark, a snowstorm was raging, and he was isolated from any protection if someone with bad intentions came to his house. Even so, he didn't hesitate one moment to invite me in, and get me close to the old woodstove for warmth.

This was Gabe, always serving others, always receiving gladly what God sent his way. It was also one of those secrets of the Kingdom of Heaven he had discovered. The Secret of *Divine Orchestration*, he often called it. I asked him what he meant. We were sitting on his porch one evening having a cup of his wonderful coffee when he leaned back in his chair, took his customary pause to collect his thoughts, and answered my question.

"Divine Orchestration," he answered, "is the rhythm and direction of God, as He weaves His plans together in a person's life. He brings people together with divine appointments so that we can contribute to His plans when He points to us to play our part. As we learn to walk with Him and trust Him, God asks us to gladly receive what He brings our way, and be patient with the process that comes with it. Why, when you knocked on my door, and I saw you on my porch in that snowstorm looking like a wet, nearly frozen corpse, I knew in my heart God had just pointed to me to play my part in His plan to help you. That's an example of *Divine Orchestration.*"

Man, was this a true statement! That stormy night was the beginning of a major transition in my life, in going from theoretical "believism" to experiential trust. It was an answer to my years of praying about going deeper in my faith. Even so, it was a large pill to swallow during the last few hours of the day.

When I entered Gabe's farmhouse, I somehow felt as if my spiritual journey would begin to make sense, and it would be the wisdom of Gabe, God would use to make it clear. I had been brought to a place I had never been before, and to a man I had never met and had very little in common with. But, I can see now it was part of the *Divine Orchestration* Gabe was talking about.

On the porch that night with him, I continued to seek Gabe's wisdom about the subject and rapidly, with enthusiasm asked, "How far reaching is it, Gabe? How far back does God's *Divine Orchestration* go back in our lives? How does our rebellion play a part? How about man's will and choices versus God's sovereignty? How about …?" and then he interrupted me.

Gabe leaned back, laughed, and said, "Hold your horses there, son! There's a lot of mystery to consider about God and His ways, and it takes time. But, that's the journey you are on isn't it? It's a mysterious journey with God of the Universe. Don't you think it will take a lifetime, even an eternity to understand the answers to those questions? You can't find answers to them simply by my explanations, or from others. We help you down your path. But ultimately you will understand, or simply trust the mysteries, because God is orchestrating your understanding and drawing you nearer to Him."

Gabe paused and began again, "I can share with you my experiences with God, and some of them you might be able to identify with. But the King deals with us all differently, in order to give us an understanding that can sink all the way down from our minds to our hearts, and not just get hung up in our brains. He doesn't want me to simply instruct you to live like me, or see things only as I do; otherwise, you will be missing out on your own unique, eternal perspective He gives to you. He wants you to learn for yourself, from Him. The best thing I can do for you is to live my life with Jesus, and passionately love and worship Him by serving you, while we are on our journey together."

This was Gabe, the master of giving me just enough information to make me hungry for more. It was frustrating for me sometimes, and I came away scratching my head more than once, because he wouldn't spoon-feed me the answers. He didn't want to tell me what to believe or how to see things. I had to always go back to Scripture and dig into it like a treasure hunter, in order to fill in those missing pieces. He knew where it would take me, and the conclusions I would come to.

But, he wanted it to be between the Lord and me, and something I discovered with God's guidance. He was always available to reinforce and encourage me, and to challenge and reprove me. But, he would not shortcut my discipleship process. If he had done so, I would always have been dependent on him rather than God, and I would have not been able to grow spiritually after he died.

Gabe told me, "A large part of the Body of Christ has become spiritually lazy and anemic because many of our church leaders are just too good at spoon-feeding their flocks. They give them a counterfeit form of discipleship in telling them what they are to believe, and how to practice it. These leaders fail to understand the

18

dynamics of what happens to a life when the Lord shows up because someone is 'self-feeding' in God's word, instead of someone 'spoon-feeding' them."

He was extremely passionate about this.

"The truth is," Gabe went on, "we can't really disciple another person. It is God Who truly disciples a man or woman. We play our part by revealing hindrances from God's Word that show someone why he is distant from God. But, the giving up of those hindrances is a decision each individual must make. For those who are willing to forfeit those hindrances, they are allowed closer proximity to Christ in an abiding relationship with Him, and it is in such close proximity to Him their lives are transformed. The Holy Spirit disciples each of His children in His own way, for a purpose that only He can see."

As if to put an exclamation point on his words, Gabe leaned closer to me and said, "Remember this: True transformation in a person's life comes only one way, and it is by proximity to Christ. The closer we live with Him, the more like Him we become. It is not by the performance of good works and the number of programs we go through that change us. It is by our lives abiding in Him and He in us that we change and become like Him. There is no other way!"

I had to will my thoughts away from our conversation and back to the present time as I continued to examine the farm. The house and barn were in good, structural condition. They were still solid, although both in need of a coat of paint. The vines had roamed free for several years, so they had to be rooted out first. I was glad that Gabe's old Ford 8N tractor was included with the sale of the property, for it was in good running condition. This alone would provide a lot of assistance in cleaning up the place.

I was still in the honeymoon period after purchasing the property from Gabe's kids. It wasn't that they didn't want to keep it, for they all adored their Daddy and Mama, and had many great memories of growing up on the farm. They also had some memories that were not so good, because it isn't glorious when it comes to doing backbreaking chores. The days can be long and hard. Little wonder they all became professionals, and moved away from the hard life they had growing up.

It had become a dilemma for Gabe's children as to what to do with the old home place, because they all lived a long distance, and had young families and careers to manage. They simply didn't have the time to oversee the place and prevent its ruination. They tried their best for over four years, but the fact is the place required a lot of catch-up maintenance, and they couldn't provide it. The distance and inconvenience were just too great for them.

Because it was a constant emotional load to carry, they wanted and needed to sell the farm. However, they did not want to give it up to just anyone. When I approached them with my desire to buy and restore it for a private retreat place for myself, family and friends, which included them, they also felt a *Divine Orchestration* had been arranged. They had their dilemma solved by my taking over the place and taking care of it. It was worked out for Dottie and me to purchase the farm, house, barn and all their contents and equipment at a very reasonable price. We were now the owners of Gabe's Farm, and it would always be referred to as such.

I walked over to the large barn and inspected it. "They sure don't build them like they did when this one was built," I thought. In my walk through the barn, I didn't see any signs of rot or termites. In fact, the solid timbers forming the barn's framework had aged in such a way that they were rock hard. The old tractor had been jacked up off the ground so the tires wouldn't rot. Gabe always kept his tools and other items around the place in good shape. That's why I knew there would be few surprises to face when I bought it.

In addition, it had only the basic necessities that would rarely break or wear out. Gabe once told me the best signature he could ever sign would be to his work. He wanted his work to always honor the Lord, no matter how mundane it might appear. Everywhere I looked on the old farm place had Gabe's "signature" of care and the quality was obvious. Everything the old man did spoke of the Lord's presence in his life.

In my continued inspection, I was delighted to see a generous supply of farm tools I would need for bringing the farm back from its overgrown condition. The last few years had taken its toll on me as far as my ability to work alone and to muscle a lot of tasks. Having a tractor, winches and other leveraging tools would be helpful assets to work with.

As I continued my walk through the fields, more memories flooded my thoughts. One in particular floated to the surface as I remembered sharing with Gabe that I was ready to begin my spiritual pilgrimage in earnest. He looked at me with joyful eyes, coupled with a concern making me know he was about to make a serious statement. "Do not be surprised or frightened by what you must face as a result of your decision. You will be tested in your resolve. But, this testing is necessary in order to become the man God wants to make of you."

I asked him, "Gabe, will it be painful?"

"I don't know," Gabe replied, "for all tests are designed for what is planned. They will be challenging, for sure. But, I can also assure you they will be things you will look back on and understand why they were necessary. You will make it through these tests, and you will be transformed into a man after God's own heart as a result. This in itself will make it worthwhile for you. But, you will be tested in areas that will challenge your fears, until they are delivered over to God, and you find peace with them."

I didn't understand at the time what the tests would be, until I now look back and see what happened the four years since Gabe's death. It was only the beginning of some very difficult tests, as my "Elijah" was removed from me, and I had to face life without him.

I looked at the surrounding buildings, including "Hotel Raccoon," the old outhouse Gabe nicknamed after I had my encounter with its resident raccoon while attempting to use it. He never let me live it down. Every time he would greet me on the front porch of the house, he would wave at the old outhouse, begin laughing and ask me, "Have you said hello to your old friend over there?"

I guess it was quite a sight to see a man trying to run out of the old outhouse with his paints to his knees, and tripping through its door. What was really funny was the disgust the raccoon showed, as he looked at me and then went back to his home underneath the privy.

Later, Gabe asked me with a twinkle in his eyes, "That old feller was pretty impatient with you, don't you think?" Then he started his belly laugh all over again as if he were seeing it for the first time. Yes, the joke was on me, but it was well worth the music of laughter that came to my ears from the old man. I couldn't help it. He always got me going. We laughed together a lot.

I made my way to the porch of the farmhouse not knowing what I would see after being away from it so long. I was concerned someone could have broken into the house and stolen some of its furniture and things. However, I saw no signs of a break-in. It was as if Gabe had simply walked out of the house, except for some new dust and wasp's nests.

I unlocked the door and stepped into the house. The smell of fireplaces and stale air greeted me. In the dim light I could see all the furniture was still there and in place. Nothing had been disturbed. It was all the same. Seeing it this way brought a sigh of relief. "God kept it safe," I whispered to myself.

I opened some windows to let in fresh air, and continued my walk through the house. In the kitchen, Old Bessie, the huge, cast-iron, wood stove, stood proudly in the center of the room. Many a good cup of coffee and meals were enjoyed on, and around, the old stove. It was a lifesaver for me. When I first enjoyed her, I was wringing wet from my fall through the ice, and Gabe brought me into his house to get warm by her while he found some dry clothes for me to wear. The coffee and warmth I felt from the woodstove, while the snowstorm blew outside, was magical. I watched Gabe that night cook on her, and came to realize I was seeing a lost art being used.

During the following visits I made with him, Gabe allowed me to try my hand in preparing a meal on her. It took a while, but I finally got the knack of opening and closing the vents to regulate the heat. It was an art the old man passed on to me, and now I would have the opportunity to use the old stove again. I was excited about the meals I would prepare on her.

Now, my wife was not as excited as I was about owning a primitive retreat house. But, I was sure she would come around when she got the full effect of a winter night, with blazing fires in the fireplaces, and patchwork quilts on the feather mattresses. I was sure the smell old Bessie provided from the wood in her fire pits, and the aroma of food being cooked on her, would turn my modern matron's heart. I had planned to serve her like Gabe served me, so that she would have a treat every time she came with me.

As I look back, I can declare my plans worked, for she now loves the place as much as I do. Our children are all grown and married with children. Gabe's farm has become special for all of us to gather together in the summers. It's a real treat for all of us to go to the swimming hole behind the house on a hot summer day and swim in the cold, clear water. And on a cool, fall night, it's a joy to have the grandchildren together, and take them hay riding on the wagon behind the tractor, while their parents laze on the porch. The magic of this place captivates us all.

But, there is more to it than the simplicity of life and nostalgia. There is a spirit of harmony lying within the valley one can sense if he or she would slow down long enough to absorb it.

The first day being the proud owner of the farm was coming to a close. I would go back to the city, make arrangements to be away for two weeks, and return a few days later. Then I would begin the long, but joyful, process of getting the old place in order. Little did I know God had a few surprises when I returned that would continue to reinforce the *Divine Orchestration.*

In the house I also saw that Gabe's clothes, his hat, the spatter-ware plates, cups and saucers, the furniture, even his Bible, were where he always placed them. These were precious items, even treasures to his children. But, they are also things they thought needed to stay with the house. We agreed that I would never give them away or sell them, but would use them as Gabe had used them, which was to serve those who God brings through the doors of the house. I continued in my amazement that the property had been left undisturbed the last several years. In this day of frequent vandalism and theft, it was a miracle Gabe's property had been left alone.

I now understood the strange feeling I had felt when I drove up to the old house. I realize I am returning to my home, even though I had not grown up here. I was destined for this place. I also sensed there was still more for me to learn, and it would unfold in a carefully laid out process.

Little did I realize at the time, there were ordinary people in the valley that had their own amazing stories and would impact me as much as Gabe's story. Their life stories and wisdom would reveal even more *Kingdom Secrets*, and add to the foundation I had received from Gabe's wisdom. That day was only the beginning of magical days for myself, and anyone who visited with people living in Gabe's Valley.

There was also something else. Out of the corner of my eye I caught a glimpse of the back and shoulders of the biggest man I had ever seen. I could tell he had been standing in the shadow of a tree at the edge of the property watching me, and when I looked in his direction, he quickly turned and walked away. He was rough in appearance, with his worn denim overalls. I couldn't see him very clearly, but what I could see sent a chill down my spine as I realized the immense damage he could bring to someone he didn't like.

In a moment, the magical embrace the farm had given me during the day was challenged by a new concern with a valley resident who could be a problem. Whatever I saw was big enough to break me in half, and a nagging feeling began to creep into my thoughts because of the immense size and sinister appearance of this man.

CHAPTER THREE

The Secret of
Divine Perspective

I arranged the next two weeks of my schedule to allow me to go back to the farm to begin the massive amount of clean up and neglected maintenance which were needed. My wife joined me after the first week, so I was alone when I started my project.

A typical day included a large breakfast at the general store a few miles down the road, a snack lunch and some kind of canned soup at night. By evening, I was so tired I didn't want to stoke up Bessie's fires, and besides, there was no firewood. My plan was to cut down some of the dead trees on the property, drag their large limbs and trunks to the house, split the wood and make a convenient woodpile for cooking and keeping fires going in the fireplaces, which included Bessie.

The first part of the week was dedicated to pulling out vines and cutting weeds, using Gabe's old Ford tractor and its brush cutter. Later in the week, I planned to use new firewood to cook a great meal on Old Bessie. The days and nights were warm and pleasant, so no fires in the fireplaces were required.

My days went as expected. The tractor performed flawlessly. My enthusiasm drove me to start early and finish late in the afternoon. A quick bath in the cold stream behind the house revived me and started my evening of rest and reflection. The satisfaction I experienced at day's end brought a tranquil appreciation of my health and the simple joy of working with my hands. Seeing the property take shape was an encouragement to a man who had spent most of his life in the city in a job that required more of his mind than his muscles. I guess "brought into balance" would be the right description of the effect I was feeling.

It was after my meal that I would take a large glass of iced tea with me and settle into one of the two rocking chairs on the front porch. I liked to read through Gabe's Bible in the remaining light of day. When it got too dark, I would move to his chair and reading lamp inside the house. I didn't feel that I had invaded his privacy, only benefited from his insight as I read the many comments and questions he had written in the margins of the old Bible.

Each night I would start my time in God's Word, and then finish our communication by praying back to Him those things I read and how they applied to my life. Gabe had shown to me a *Kingdom Secret* with how to converse with God. He called it, "getting a *Divine Perspective*." He told me the Lord would have His children develop their communication with Him by reading His Word and allowing Him to speak to us through it, while applying those passages to our lives. We should then answer Him by praying back our response. He talks and we listen, and then we talk and He listens.

I have been learning to converse with God through this practice. Before hearing Gabe's wisdom, I was bound up by rote and habit in my prayers and they were ineffective. I also thought I was missing something big, even though I was actively praying. I often mentioned and requested the same things in my prayers without thinking about what I was asking. I could see as a father, myself, I would be insulted if any of my family only saw me as a means to an end, and wasn't really interested in what I had to say. I never made the connection with how self-centered I was in my prayers, and how I was hurting my own devotional life, until hearing Gabe's perspective. I must also say that a *Divine Perspective* can become a "divine wrestling match" with God, as well, as was the case during that first week with me.

I finished reading some passages from the Bible and was ready to converse with God about what I had read because the verses seemed to hit the target of a concern I had about the huge man I continued to get a glimpse of during the day. His behavior seemed odd to me when I would notice him watching me from a distance. It was creepy!

That night I had just read a passage where Jesus had taught when we feed the hungry, give drink to the thirsty, provide clothes to the needy and invite strangers into our home to care for them, we have in fact have done it to Him. Jesus explained when we have done these things to the least of these people, we have done it to Him. It was with this Scripture in mind, I left my chair and walked to the front yard of the house to find the *Divine Perspective* I felt God wanted to give to me.

It was a brilliantly lit night as the stars were out in full effect. Since there were no streetlights to contend with, the necessary backdrop of a black sky caused a plethora of stars and planets to come to my view. I felt as if I could reach out and touch them. These would be objects I would never have noticed before. Almost at the same time when I looked at the night-time sky, I realized God was speaking to my heart and saying to me:

> *"Removing distractions and having a different point of view can show you things that are hidden treasures, just like these stars."*

Now when I say, "God speaks to me," understand His "words" spoken to my heart must pass through the grid of His living Word, which I have absorbed from the Bible. When I read passages in the

Bible that "speak to me," I intellectually receive the words and contemplate their context and meaning. But, when I engage God's words into my life's framework and circumstances, and apply them to my life, He then "speaks" to my heart. The more I commit to the study and application of His Word to my heart and soul, the more familiar I am with His Voice.

Jesus said His people would know His voice. When my King speaks to me through His written Word, and I apply it to my life's circumstances and decisions I must make, He speaks to my heart and He gives me direction. It is at this point I have a *Divine Perspective* for dealing with a situation or problem.

That night, I had a sneaking suspicion, because of past experiences, God was setting me up for one of His *Divine Perspective* talks. I didn't particularly like where this conversation was headed. So I protested in an audible voice to what He was speaking to my heart about. (The Lord was dealing with me about the big man I kept seeing in the woods.)

I'm glad nobody heard me pray:

> *"But Lord, have you seen that guy? He makes two of me, and he could chew me up for breakfast if he had a mind to. Surely he's not one of the "least" of Yours, is he Lord? Is there someone smaller and less creepy who I can serve?"*

As I spoke these things out loud, I hoped no one was watching me, for I was pacing back and forth in front of the farmhouse, and talking to the Lord as if He were sitting on the porch. Talk about being concerned over someone's behavior? I was sure this conversation would look a little suspicious, even to the behemoth who had been stalking me all day. Even so, I continued my conversation with God. Before I could speak, He spoke.

> *"Trust Me, I will keep you safe."*

The words were encouraging.

"OK Lord, OK, I'll do it. I'll welcome him into the house if he ever comes over."

Thinking I would agree with the Lord's request and try to change the subject, I quickly acquiesced to the instructions I heard coming to me. But the Voice didn't stop.

"You go to him."

Staying on subject, I replied,

"But what else can I do? He looks like a Bigfoot walking around here. There's something that's just not right about him, and there's no telling how he'll react to me. Maybe he's afraid I'll find his moonshine still, or something worse."

God said again,

"Trust Me."

The Voice continued to speak to my heart, and I had to protest,

"But why do I always have to lead out, Lord? Is there anyone else You can send?"

The Voice persisted,

"Trust Me. You are the one for him, and I am sending you to him."

Then I changed tactics with my negotiation by saying,

"I know a better idea. Let me grow some watermelons, and when they get ripe, unless he steals them, I'll take him some. That way it will seem more natural."

I was bartering as best I could while hoping for more time. It wasn't working, for how can you negotiate with Someone who already knows your next move?

He kept speaking to me. You can guess what He was asking me by my response to His questions.

> *"Yes, Lord, I know others have served me, and have taken quite a risk in doing so, even the man whose farm I'm standing on. But ...?"*

> *"Yes, Lord, I understand You are asking me to do it for You, and when I serve someone else I'm really doing it to You. But ...?"*

> *"Yes, Lord, I remember your words when one has been given much, much is required, but can't it also mean ...?"*

> *"Yes, Lord, I understand ... but Lord ... I guess the truth is ... I really don't understand ... and I need You to help me see things through Your heart and eyes."*

As I slowed down and began to listen closely to the Scriptures I had read for years in His Word, and let His voice speak to my heart, His answers to my questions began to flow to me.

I heard:

> *"My son, you cannot really know this man by simply looking at his appearance, or see the wounds that have fractured his life. I can see his heart, and I know his thoughts. I know his needs, as none other can. I am asking you to do this for Me. I could demand it of you, for I have the right to do so. I could even allow guilt to be your persuader. But I will not. It is not to him or for him that you serve. It is to Me and for Me. When you do this, you will also share in My view of him. Trust Me to make you My hands and voice to him as you go. We will go after this man together. I also want to bless you. I will do this by*

including you in the blessing I will give to him through you. Will you allow yourself to be an answered prayer for someone, and allow Me to bless someone as you serve Me? If you do not die to yourself in things such as this, you cannot be alive in the new life I want to give you. Have you forgotten My intention is to make you into the man I revealed you would become if you obey Me?"

This last statement pierced the shell around my heart like a spear, and cracked it open to drive home my King's personal request to me. At the same time He spoke this to me, I remembered the vision of several years before when He showed me the man I would become. I could have no other response.

I answered,

"Father, I now see this through Your perspective, as I should have all along. I abandon myself to You, for Your purpose. I ask You now to show me my next steps. I will follow You wherever you lead, even to the man who frightens me."

Then came the King's reassuring voice,

"Just make yourself available. Wait and watch, and you will know what to do next. Trust Me, for I will be right by your side."

Little did I realize, as I wrestled with God that night, someone would indeed be receiving a great blessing as a result of my obeying God's voice. There is no doubt in my mind what followed could have been missed because of a cold heart of disobedience and prejudice on my part. I would have hindered a *Divine Orchestration* that would reach the heart of a man who was greatly misunderstood, and in great pain. In reaching out to him, God would also reach out to the heart of this man who needed his faith to grow outside his comfort zone.

When I agreed to abandon my perspective of the man, and look through God's point of view, my next steps in a *Divine Dispatchment* began to unfold. God would reach out to this other man through me. But in doing so, He would help me become the man I had always desired to be.

CHAPTER FOUR

The Secret of
Divine Dispatchment

W hat a good night's sleep!" was the first thing out of my mouth while rising from the feather mattress bed I had slept on. The hard work and my removal from the sensory overload masses of people, heavy traffic and awful TV programming bring, allowed me to have a restful night's sleep. I was looking forward to another great day of work, preceded by the lumberjack breakfast waiting for me at the café a few miles from the farm.

There is a little country store in the valley that has about anything practical you can want or need. But, you will only find about one or two of each item. If you need more, you'll have to wait about a week for the next shipment or go to the nearest town 20 miles away. Most people are willing to wait, or as most farmers do from necessity, build it. Some very creative engineering has taken place on farms because of time and need, or not having the money to pay for it. It is likely still prevalent in the valley, for the community is a throwback in time to at least 50 years. Besides, most people don't like leaving the valley, except those like Gabe's children who grow up and move to the cities to get away from the harsh life of farming.

The general store is the center of the valley's commerce. The 90-year-old building houses the grocery and hardware store, the post office and Maude Mae's Grill. The voluntary fire department's 1960 fire truck is parked in its own garage behind the store. A gas pump is out front, and diesel fuel is sold from a tank on the side of the building. The first thing greeting a shopper going into the store, is typically two or three old men sitting on a wooden bench whittling a cedar stick, and chewing tobacco at a very leisurely pace.

Inside the store the look of an antique building has remained. It has wooden floors with an amber hue due to oiled sawdust being used when it is swept. The oil helps with the dust and also protects the wood from wet, muddy boots coming from a field. A pressed tin ceiling hangs from a ceiling 20 feet above the floor. A beautiful, old, cash register no less than 100 years old, sits proudly on the checkout counter. A large, potbelly stove provides a little extra heat and a lot of nostalgia, as it supplements the gas heaters against the walls.

Canned foods and breads are on shelves lining the walls. Pots and pans are placed on a second level of shelves, requiring a ladder or a stick with a hook on the end to access them. Hardware items are separated in the back portion of the large room. The seed rack and planting supplies also have a special space in the store. Milk and frozen items are in the three refrigerators everyone calls "Frigidaires," even though they are another brand. Most of the people in the valley call a refrigerator a Frigidaire, and a soft drink a Coke. It can be an orange Coke, or a grape Coke, but it is still a variety of Coke as far as they are concerned. They seem to understand the difference with root beer, however. Likely because no one has ever tasted an orange root beer, or would ever admit it.

Fresh produce, brought in daily by farmers, is stacked in bins below the front windows. Glass cabinets house sweets and candies, and lure every child to drool over the tasty treats. Small handprints and stains from children's mouths lay semitransparent on the glass, proving the marketability of candy that can be seen will create a crying child. But, it is kept out of reach until a parent or grandparent gives in to the cries for a piece of candy.

To the side of the store, Maude Mae has her café. It can be accessed through its own front door or through an opening through the wall from the general store. Red and white-checkered vinyl tablecloths cover each of the five tables. Maude cooks, and a fifty-ish woman named Pearl waits tables. Like so many waitresses in the American South, Pearl calls everyone "Hon," "Sugar" or "Dear." Sure enough, she cheerfully greeted me with, "Now what can I get for you today, Hon?"

I ordered my customary breakfast and several cups of coffee. While doing so, a man a little older than me I had come to realize was the owner of the store, introduced himself.

"You bought Old Gabe's place, didn't you," he said while holding out a large, calloused, farmer's hand. "Name's Burt. I'm Maude Mae's husband, and we own the store. But, I guess you can say Maude runs it, and I take orders from her."

Without my answer, the cheerful Burt stated, "You got a lot of work to do, neighbor. Gabe's place has seen better years, but you got a good plot of land when you got that place. A lot of us would have liked to have gotten it, but I understand Gabe's kids wanted you to have it, so that it would be protected and used like Gabe used it. We're all mighty glad about it, for that old man blessed a lot of people. I know one thing for sure, my daddy, Burt Senior, and some of the other old timers around here, say there was a time the little, 80-acre plot of land you own fed everyone in this valley. The families who lived here wouldn't have made it through some mighty lean times without Gabe and his farm getting us through it."

Before I could ask more about his last comment, someone called Burt to help him with something, and he had to excuse himself by saying, "We'll catch up more later. Welcome to the valley," as he hurried off.

I hadn't heard the story Burt was talking about. I was aware of the neighbor who broke his leg while trying to burn down Gabe's barn, and he and his family were taken care of by Gabe. The man's son had told the story at Gabe's funeral. But, this was something else, even more intriguing. I sensed there was more to this story, and I was determined to find out about it if I could find someone who knew the details first hand. They would have to be old, and have a good memory, which most of the time didn't exactly go together.

I finished my breakfast and paid Pearl while introducing myself to the busy Maude Mae. I chose to walk through the general store on the way out to see if I could spot something I might need for my work. While doing so, I heard Burt say, "Now, Aunt Matte, you know it's too hot for you to be walking home today with your groceries. Let me fix Elmer's flat tire, and I'll run you home in about an hour."

"No, Burt," the elderly woman responded. "I have a cake in the oven and I can't wait," as she began to walk out the front door.

I felt Burt needed some help with Aunt Mattie, so I volunteered, "Burt, do you want me to run her home? I can leave right now."

Burt looked at me and nodded his head saying yes while following the elderly woman out the door. "Aunt Mattie, meet the man who bought Gabe's place. He said he'd give you a ride. Now you go ahead and let him serve you. You serve everybody else all the time, and you've got to be on the receiving end sometimes yourself."

Aunt Mattie slowly turned and looked at me. She had bright blue eyes with a little sparkle in them. She winked at me and spoke toward me while she was really speaking to Burt. "Burt, you act like I'm 100 years old and can't walk myself home."

Burt replied, "If I'm not mistaken, we are only a few months from our 85th birthday, aren't we, Aunt Mattie?" Burt said while also winking at me. Then he said to me, "Now you take real good care of Aunt Mattie. Anyone who is 20 years old or older born in this valley, had Aunt Mattie's hands on them first thing when they came into this world. The doctor lived so far away, Aunt Mattie became the mid-wife of the valley. The doctor said she handled things better than he could, and there was none better. So, she's mighty special to all of us."

"She's in good hands," I replied. Then to Aunt Mattie, I asked, "May I take those grocery bags and help you into my truck?"

Aunt Mattie took my arm and followed me to the truck. She lived about a mile down the road, so it was not inconvenient to take her home. Since I needed a valley historian to find out more about Burt's story on Gabe, I reasoned I might have been pointed to the right person.

On the way to Aunt Mattie's house, she made it clear to me she was only a few months away from her 84th birthday, and she would have to have a little talk with Burt about keeping his facts straight. I could tell she was a little sensitive about her age.

She told me she had no natural children of her own, but had hundreds who would claim she was family to them, and this was the reason everyone in the valley called her "Aunt." She had lost her husband when she was in her forties because of a tractor accident, and as a result provided for herself by raising a little vegetable patch, taking in sewing, and serving as the mid-wife in the valley up until 20 years before. She was sharp as a tack and enjoyable to be around. There was no loss of her mental faculties because of her age. On the contrary, I sensed a wisdom that would be a joy to learn from.

I was later to learn Aunt Mattie was a prayer warrior who always pointed a troubled person to the right place, which is toward Jesus. When a prayer request went to Aunt Mattie, she took it very seriously, and she stayed with it until something began to show her prayer was being answered. When Aunt Mattie spotted something that needed God's help for one of her "children," she stayed on her knees until help was delivered. Although I felt Aunt Mattie would help me find something out about Gabe's story, I didn't realize at the time I had also stepped right into one of her prayers for someone else. I would become an answer to a prayer she had been praying for a long time.

It began to take shape when she invited me to her porch for lemonade, and to do her a "slight favor." I also was to learn there were very few favors she would ask of anyone that could be refused. Doing her a favor would also become part of an answered prayer she was involved with. She and I would become fast friends, and she would be a continual resource of *Kingdom Secrets* to me.

While I waited on the front porch of Aunt Mattie's small, clapboard house, I looked around at the neat order of her flower and vegetable gardens. The gardens were small, but would be very productive as spring moved into summer. The dirt was loamy and well tilled, with rows ready for planting. A rabbit-proof fence surrounded the vegetable garden. Chickens pecked in the yard looking for worms, bugs or seeds to eat. Aunt Mattie rattled drink glasses inside the house while she squeezed lemon for the lemonade. I relaxed and enjoyed the moment.

A few minutes later, Aunt Mattie brought glasses of lemonade through the front door. She took a seat in the rocking chair next to mine, and handed me one of the drink glasses. I waited for her to compose herself and take a drink first, being loyal to my Southern upbringing of "ladies first." Then I took a long drink of her wonderful mixture. "Just right!" I declared.

Aunt Mattie led out, "So you bought Gabe's farm, did you? Tell me how you got to know Gabe and come to buy his place."

I answered her by giving her a rapid review of my introduction of Gabe, and how our friendship developed over the next few years. I shared with her why Gabe's children let us buy the property, and how I planned to use it. I told her a little about my dream for using it in various ministry opportunities. I brought her up-to-date on my work on the farm, and my plans for the spring and summer. I did most of the talking so she could get to know me. But, what I really wanted to hear was her background. Before I could get to it, she moved quickly to her "slight favor" of me. Even though I am sure I fell into her prayer agenda, I was surprised to learn she had also fallen into my prayer of the night before, about the massive man who I continued to see at the edge of my property.

"Young man," she began, "I will pray for you and the ministry that will unfold for you at Gabe's farm. But, I ask you to start your ministry immediately by reaching out to the most misunderstood individual I have ever known."

"What can I do Aunt Mattie?" I asked.

"There is a man who lives near you I helped birth 30 years ago today. His mother and father had been married many years, and were childless. They had given up all hope a baby would ever bless their lives. Therefore, it was quite the surprise when she conceived at such a late age. Because of her health, the doctor told her to abort the child, for it was dangerous for her, and the child would likely have severe problems. Neither she nor the father would ever consider doing this, mainly because the mother believed God had done a miraculous thing that needed to be left alone, and to allow His plan to unfold. The father just trusted his wife's decision."

Aunt Mattie leaned back in her rocker and took a small swallow of lemonade before continuing her story.

"These people were like everyone else in the valley, uncomplicated and hardworking. But, Ned's mother had a faith that taught us all a great lesson about trust and hope in Jesus. She believed God had a special plan for her baby. From day one, she began to earnestly pray for the child in her womb. She pleaded for God to keep the child safe as she laid both their lives before God. She asked Him to take her life if needed, but to take the child by hand, and lead the baby throughout its life."

Aunt Mattie slowly turned her chair so that she could look me straight in my eyes. Her eyes, blue with fire, looked deep into my soul, as the look of one who has compassion burning within. A mere glance of her eyes sent a hidden message to me that something serious was about to be spoken. Tears formed in her eyes, and her square on look made me realize I had better listen up. She had my full attention.

"The night the baby was born, I was asked to go to their house. There was a terrible storm, and a flood had washed the bridge out between the city and their house. The doctor was running late, so he sent word to me to go and be with her. He tried for several hours to get to their home for the birth, but he just wasn't able to get across the river. He had to travel many miles upstream to find a bridge not closed by the flood."

Aunt Mattie struggled with her next words. "The labor lasted almost 12 hours. The baby was breached, and I did everything I knew to do to turn it. With every contraction, she would cry out, 'Save my baby, Lord! Just save my baby!' I think she knew something was wrong from the start."

After taking another sip of lemonade to clear her throat and calm her emotions, Aunt Mattie continued her story:

"In the last few hours before the birth, I began to detect her breathing was changing and her pulse was weakening. The phone lines were down, so I couldn't talk to her doctor. He would have likely taken the baby with a C-section. I wasn't qualified to do it, and at her age I just couldn't risk it. So, all I could do was pray. The doctor finally arrived. He opened her up and took the baby. Unfortunately, the mother's heart just gave out. She had one look at her baby, weakly smiled, and then passed."

I sensed Aunt Mattie had been carrying a burden for this child a long time, and the fact she couldn't do anything to save the mother. She didn't say anything for several minutes, so I respected her silence and simply held her hand. In a short while, the distance normally standing between strangers was bridged, and two souls were joined with compassion — mine for her, and her for the child she had been praying about over 30 years. God had given me enough experience with the way He uses lives to touch other lives with His love to know I was now within a *Divine Dispatchment*, which would roll out before me.

"Aunt Mattie," I tenderly asked, "Who is the man you speak of?" I think I knew the answer before my question rolled off my tongue.

"He lives alone next to your place in a run down house. He's a very big man. You will know him when you see him, for he might be described as rough looking," she replied.

I immediately thought Aunt Mattie's last comment was an understatement, for he was much more than "rough looking." I've been around rough looking men, and this fellow would make any of them run for cover. It didn't surprise me when she told me who it was. I suspected the perspective the Lord gave me the night before was a precursor to what would be taking place. True to His last words to me to, "Wait and watch," God was showing me my next step to take in reaching out to the big man next door.

Aunt Mattie continued, "Today is Sonny Boy's birthday, and I'm baking him a cake. His real name is Ned, but I've always called him 'Sonny Boy.'"

"Does Ned have friends and family nearby?" I asked.

"Well, that's the problem. I'm about the only one now since Gabe is gone," she answered. "Sonny Boy has had a hard life. He lost his mother at birth. His father was a hard, proud, unsociable man. When we tried to help him with his new son, he refused. He felt it was his duty to raise the boy alone. So Sonny Boy grew up without a mother, other family members and friends. Since I was there at his birth, the father allowed me to have some contact with him. But nobody else was permitted. Consequently, Sonny Boy has grown up isolated except for his father and me."

She continued, "Sonny Boy has always been big. When he was 10 years old, he looked to be 18, and could work like a grown man. He worked along side his father cutting and hauling timber when he wasn't in school. By 12 years old, he had to drop out of school, because his father was paralyzed from a stroke and couldn't work. The old man would ride with Sonny Boy in the cab of the log truck while Sonny Boy would cut and haul the timber back to the sawmill. By 15, the boy was doing everything from cooking for them, to doing all the work to provide for them. When the old man died, Sonny Boy just continued life alone, and it's been that way ever since."

Aunt Mattie rested a minute before continuing. While she did, I reflected on the life story of Ned, and quite frankly didn't see how he could have made it this far without having some major issues in his life. I couldn't see how in the world I would be able to help this man, for his needs would, no doubt, be way beyond my abilities. Before I could think any more about it, Aunt Mattie interrupted my thoughts.

"The old man didn't have much to leave Sonny Boy except the shack he lives in, a beat up truck for hauling logs, and a fear of the world outside his predictable environment. It's not that he has anything to fear, for he could certainly take care of himself. Rather, it's an awkwardness and shyness around people. He's been alone so long, and isolated from interaction with people, he has just not developed socially. Gabe was about the best thing that happened to Sonny Boy. But, he didn't let Gabe into his life until several years had passed after the father died. Even Gabe couldn't break him out of his shell. Just when there seemed to be a little headway, Gabe did like every other person who got close to Sonny Boy did ... he died. I've been praying for years God would send to Sonny Boy someone who would build on the foundation Gabe had already begun. I am praying this man is you."

Now, the first thing that came to my mind was, "If Gabe couldn't break though to Ned, how in the world could I?" Even so, I could see God was leading me to a *Divine Dispatchment* by having prepared the way for many years with Aunt Mattie's prayers, and Gabe opening the door. I have often felt God is not early enough to satisfy my impatience, but it is always proven to me that He is never too late in answering my prayers. I could see Aunt Mattie had been faithfully praying for Ned for over 30 years, and I began to understand I was now going to play my part in God's *Divine Orchestration*. "Paul planted and Apollos watered," came to mind, as I mentally screened a rapidly moving process through Scripture. It seemed to make sense to me God would bring the right people together for a job He had in mind. I still had no idea what my part would be. My King has never required me to understand, but only obey. I did feel comforted that understanding would unfold as I stepped into His *Divine Dispatchment* that He had "divinely orchestrated."

I said goodbye to Aunt Mattie and told her I would be back in touch, for I had some questions about Gabe I wanted to ask of her.

CHAPTER FIVE

The Secret of
Divine Preparation

I left Aunt Mattie's house with a sense of duty and with a
birthday cake in hand. The cake was for Ned, and was in her
stove baking when we talked. I had originally taken her home with
the hopes of finding out about Burt's statement concerning Gabe's
farm. I understood quickly that my agenda was rewritten before I
knew what was happening. Her Southern charm, and a request
from a Southern Belle, is about as easy to turn away as a runaway
train.

However, I knew it was the right thing to do even though my
agenda was put on hold. My concern now was with how to
approach Ned. Would I go to his house on foot or by car? I didn't
want to sneak up on the big guy and surprise him. Aunt Mattie said
he was safe, but I didn't want to startle a man that big. I didn't care
how "safe" he was to Aunt Mattie, I was thinking entirely about
my own safety.

I whispered a simple prayer by saying,

"Here we go, Lord. I trust that You are going before me and are also with me to prepare the way for me."

I drove home and started to look for any road close to the farm that might lead to Ned's house. Sure enough, I spotted a two-lane trail leading through the trees. There was overgrowth on each side of the trail giving it an eerie, closed in feeling.

I followed the tunneled growth as it wound through the forest. After about a quarter mile of driving, I came to an opening in the forest. At its center stood an old, log cabin. There was also a beat-up, log-hauling truck parked close to the cabin. I could tell it was on its last miles, however, I have seen old trucks like it hauling wood that were in far worse condition. By using wire and salvaged parts from a junked vehicle, the backwoods ingenuity of an owner would keep it running somehow.

The truck being present was an indication, Ned was likely home. I looked around the rest of the place, and it was like the truck. Old tools were scattered everywhere, and a general rundown condition was obvious. Another dilapidated truck, likely a junked truck Ned scavenged parts from, sat in the corner of the clearing. Two chain saws rested on the porch and, curiously, a guitar was propped against the wall next to a rocking chair.

As I drove closer to the cabin, I could see a glass of water next to the chair, which was still rocking, as if a hasty exit was executed. I could feel my adrenalin rushing while thinking that a shotgun or rifle was aimed at me. I wanted to turn around quickly and leave the place. But, I had processed the scenario already in my mind, and there was no going back. I could only rely on God's presence and protection, and the assurance from Aunt Mattie that Ned was only shy and not dangerous.

I whispered, "Sure, Aunt Mattie. Your precious, shy, Sonny Boy has a gun aimed between my eyes right now. I wish I had you standing in front of me. I don't care if you are 84 years old. 'Do me a slight favor' you asked. You owe me for this one!"

I parked my truck within talking range of the cabin, but far enough away so I wouldn't come across too aggressively. I also parked the truck in such a way so when I opened the driver's side door, the truck was between the cabin and me, offering some protection. I opened the door and slowly eased out of the truck, and respectfully waited for movement within the cabin.

The rule of thumb I had learned when approaching a backwoods house is wait respectfully at the truck, and wait for the occupant to come to the door. They are watching and checking you out to make sure you don't threaten them in some way. Generally, there is a gun pointed at you with the safety on. In a short while they will either step through the door and talk to you, or speak though the door and talk to you, or stay silent inside the house, with the gun ready to be fired. If the silence lingers too long, it would be best to make an exit, and as quickly as possible. So, I waited for Ned to make the next move.

Inside the screened door I heard a cough, telling me that Ned was making himself known. A short while later, he spoke in a deep voice, "What you want?"

"Ned, I want to introduce myself to you. I'm your new neighbor," I quickly stated.

"I already know that. I been watchin' you since you moved in," was his reply. He didn't sound very inviting to me.

"Aunt Mattie asked me to drop by and introduce myself to you. She also gave me something to give to you. She baked a cake for your birthday, and asked me to give it to you. Can I leave it with you now?" I was doing my best to not start running down the trail back to the main road. My legs were ready to move even though my body stayed put.

"You got a cake Aunt Mattie cooked?" Ned's interest was piqued as he asked the question.

Relieved a little, I said, "Yeah, it looks mighty good, and it just came out of her oven. Still warm."

The screened door slowly opened, and the big man eased through with the smoothness and grace of a panther. He looked like an NFL defensive end, with bulging arms and shoulder muscles, a thin waste, narrow hips, and very little excess fat. His rusty-colored hair was long and matted with a beard to match. He looked in my direction and asked again, "Aunt Mattie just made the cake?" It seemed to be important to Ned.

"Yep," I replied while gaining courage. "It's still warm and ready to be eaten."

I eased into the truck, lifted the foil-wrapped cake, and showed it to Ned. I moved slowly around the truck and extended the cake to Ned who was now standing on the porch. As I got closer to him, I felt as if I were approaching a mountain gorilla that had permitted me to come close. I was permitted, but I was also very much aware I was close to a wild beast that could rip me apart whenever it pleased. At least, that's what I was feeling at the time.

Ned reached out to take the cake from me with his massive hands. However, I was surprised they were not the hands of a typical lumberjack, with a tough hide and hardened by physical work. Strangely, they were obviously strong, but they also appeared supple. The nails were clean, trimmed, and altogether looked more like the hands of an artist. I could tell Ned protected his hands for some reason. It's funny. In an instant of time, because of seeing those hands, I started to realize there were hidden things about Ned, and more to him than my first impression allowed. This made me a little more relaxed and confident that maybe he wasn't as bad as he looked.

Looking for some common ground, I asked, "Ned, do you play the guitar? I see one in the corner over there," while pointing to the instrument.

"Yeah, I play it," Ned answered.

I prayed in my mind, "Good move. Now, Lord, help me build a bridge to the big guy."

"Maybe we can jam together sometime. I play a little harmonica. In fact, tomorrow night I plan to cook some fried chicken like Gabe taught me, and I'd like to invite you over to share it with me. We can call it your birthday party."

I was surprised by my offer. I had no idea when I drove up to Ned's cabin I would later be inviting him over to my home. There was a divine work going on in my heart that reinforced my "baby steps" of obedience. I could see God's *Divine Preparation* at work, even before my own willingness to venture forward was in place. Something had awakened in me, which was lying dormant and ready to be expressed. My courage was growing as I felt God had truly dispatched me to this man, and there was a plan in place by God.

"You gonna fire up Old Bessie?" Ned asked.

I could tell by his question Ned had been in Gabe's house, and he was familiar with an invitation such as mine, which also likely had come from Gabe.

"That's my plan. As soon as I rustle up some firewood tomorrow, I'll get her going and start cooking a little before dark. I don't think I can cook as good as Gabe. But, I'll give it my best shot. Can you come over?" I asked again.

"OK. I'll bring my guitar," Ned answered. The mountain gorilla had permitted me an audience.

49

I didn't stay much longer after Ned gave his agreement. I excused myself after I told him the time he ought to show up. As I drove back to my house, taking the two-lane trail back to the main road, I felt both a spirit of relief and of excitement, because I had seen God prepare the way for my meeting with Ned.

I haven't been in many of those zones when things fall into place as if they were a natural fit, and you didn't have to do much more than show up. That's the way I was feeling. That doesn't happen often, but when it does, you know God is at work. I'm sure Aunt Mattie, *God bless her little Southern Belle manipulative heart*, was on her knees right now, praying for this connection between Ned and me. No doubt, her prayers were a powerful ingredient for seeing this scenario play out.

I still had a full day's work ahead. Since I needed firewood starting tomorrow, I thought I would haul the dead limbs and trees I had already collected to the woodpile. Tomorrow, I would cut and stack the wood, which had to be done by hand, and something I dreaded. But, it had to be done. I also planned to buy the chicken and vegetables for dinner when I went for my breakfast at Maude Mae's café.

The day worked out pretty much as I planned. As evening fell, I put together my dinner of soup and sandwiches. I was starting to get tired of canned soup for dinner, and was really looking forward to a big meal tomorrow night. I can understand why farmers generally eat three meals a day. They work so hard, and burn up so many calories, they need to replenish themselves.

I was also ready to spend time with my King under His stars. The day had been really special for me, and I just wanted to feel His presence and allow Him to speak to my heart. I felt we needed to talk. Therefore, after supper, I started our conversation as normal, by going to Gabe's Bible, letting a verse speak to my heart, and then making my way outside with a glass of iced tea. There, I would sit under His canopy of stars and gain a proper sense of awe. It is a very special way I have discovered for preparing my heart to meet with Him. Before long, I began to speak to Him about the verse and how I understood what He was saying to my heart.

> *"Jesus, I read in Gabe's Bible about Philip and the Ethiopian. Certainly, Philip might have questioned why he was being taken from a fruitful ministry in Samaria to a road in the desert, although it doesn't mention it. Maybe he was so tuned in to You, he never questioned Your directions? Maybe this is my problem? Maybe I need to be better tuned in to Your voice, and ask less questions, and just respond?"*

I paused from my prayer and looked closely at the beautiful, star-filled sky, while trying to visualize the scene of Philip approaching the chariot.

> *"Savior, I read that Philip asked the Ethiopian if he knew what he was reading. The man replied, 'How can I unless I have someone to explain it?' Is this my mission to Ned? Is my role to help him understand the work You are already doing in his life? Is it as simple as this?"*

I thought a few minutes about what I could offer Ned. There was so little we have in common. I am old enough to be his father. I have never had a disadvantaged life. I would think he would need someone trained in working with special needs people and who understood complex human needs.

> *"Lord, what can I offer Ned? I will give myself to You for Your purpose in reaching out to him. But I just don't know what I have to offer him."*

As I stilled myself, and waited for God's answer, images of Gabe's interaction with me began to unfold. Spoken to my heart were these words from the Lord:

> *"How much in common did you and My servant Gabe have? Did he not welcome you into his world, and simply serve your obvious needs? Did he not simply befriend you,*

51

and in doing so help you understand the work I had already begun in your life? Ask yourself if it was Gabe serving you out of his own abilities that filled in what was missing in your life, or was it Me working through his life as I reached out to you through him?"

This last question by the Lord helped me see the obvious answer. God had already begun His work in Ned's life, and it was my role to simply explain what was going on. I had been invited in for this purpose.

"My son, I will be with you. Do not fret over what you do not know, or if you will be prepared for my assignment. In the moment you need it, I will instruct you in what you will say or do. Enter into this mission with Me and you will see a mighty work done in Ned's life which will serve My purpose. Live with Me in a state of dependence, and My power will be made perfect in your weakness."

With God's firm assurance, I returned to the farmhouse and went to bed.

CHAPTER SIX

The Secret of
Divine Dependency

I awoke from a great sleep with a busy day ahead. The first thing on my agenda was to shop for the necessary groceries for the evening meal when I went for breakfast at the general store. Also needed were gas and oil for the chainsaw, for I had a lot of cutting and stacking of wood that was in store for me. I quickly dressed and headed down the road.

Maude Mae's Grill was busy with farmers eating their breakfast. I was just one of the guys, except they wore overalls and I was dressed in jeans and a cotton shirt. I wasn't "pure country" yet, but I realized that if I wanted to fit in with these guys, I needed to buy a pair of "overhauls," which they were called. They are actually good because they have pockets for about anything you want to hang on them.

The "real deal" farmers wear only the "overhauls," if you know what I mean. The guys say, "There is nothing between them and

God except those "overhauls." If that's what it takes, I guess I'll just have to try it. I'm not sure how my wife will take it. But, hey, I want to be the "real deal," and there's got to be a great appeal when she sees me on the tractor wearing those overhauls and knowing that there's nothing between God and me but them. How could she resist loving a guy like that?

While I was eating, Burt came up to me and asked, "How was your time with Aunt Mattie?"

"Hey Burt!" I answered and continued. "She's a nice lady, but she sure knows how to get someone to be part of her plans quick enough."

Burt laughed a laugh as if he knew exactly what I was talking about, because of personal experience I would imagine.

"Yeah, she'll get you into one of her missions, but no one I've known has ever regretted it. She has a strong prayer life, and when you're invited by her to be a helper in that prayer, most of us think we've heard the voice of God speaking to us."

"Well, I guess I have to agree," I replied. "She has me meeting with my neighbor, Ned. I was trying to figure out how I could get to know him, and before I knew it, Aunt Mattie is asking me to take a birthday cake to him."

"You talked with Sonny Boy?" Burt asked with a surprised look. "I don't think anybody around these parts has even heard his voice. He comes by for gas and oil and a few groceries, but he keeps to himself. I know one thing though. He's a scary looking dude."

"That's an understatement," I thought.

Burt continued, "Aunt Mattie has been carrying a burden for that young man ever since he was born. His father was a peculiar fellow and always felt like someone wanted to get into his business. I think he kept Ned isolated because he was afraid and suspicious of the outside world. You wouldn't even know there was a cabin back in those woods unless you were looking real hard for it. There's a bunch of people in this valley who would have helped the old man with Ned, and would have been blessed by it. But, he just wouldn't take our help. I can't imagine what it must have been like growing up with that kind of paranoia. I know one thing for sure. That old man sure did a number on his son, and we've come to think around here that Ned is unapproachable, except for Aunt Mattie. I guess you might be the answer to her prayers for that boy, after all."

I told Burt about seeing Ned several times watching me from a distance.

"There was a reason. Gabe asked Ned to watch over it in case he died, and until someone came to claim it," Burt explained. "That boy wouldn't let anybody drive up that road to Gabe's house without checking them out. It didn't take but one look at him to frighten anyone who wanted to do some bad stuff to the place. Word got around that you didn't want to show up there if Ned didn't know you. I guess he had seen you around the place several times with Gabe, and so he knew it was alright for you to be there."

I thought, "That answers the question about why the farm was left alone."

Little did I realize that God had been connecting me to Ned without my knowing it, and strangely enough, Ned had already been a blessing to me by watching over the place. I was really getting a heart for the big man. Maybe I was now starting to look at him through God's eyes and understood that I could count on His help to show me what to do.

Changing the subject, I asked, "Burt, you said something about Gabe's farm feeding the valley during some hard times. I haven't heard that story about Gabe. I wanted to talk to Aunt Mattie about it but got sidetracked by her cake and Ned. Can you tell me more about it?"

"Well, there's more to that story than Gabe just taking care of us with what his farm produced, although that's a big part of it. There was a real evil element living in this valley, and Gabe was the target of it. I was pretty young at the time, so you'll have to get Aunt Mattie settled down long enough to get her to tell you about it. I've just heard it from the old folks that Gabe was the most courageous man they'd ever seen, and he led them to freedom. Now, I don't exactly know what that means, 'leading them to freedom,' cause the old timers kept it among themselves. But there was something big, and the way I hear it, it brought on a spiritual awakening that's still going on today."

Before I could ask anything else, the "Busy Burt" had to scoot off to serve another customer in the hardware store. He said we would get coffee the next morning and chat some more. I finished my breakfast and did my grocery shopping.

Now, if you want to make a great country meal, then shopping at the general store is the place to get the fixins. I was able to buy fresh chicken, spring mustard greens, and sweet potatoes. Along with the cornbread I would be baking, I added to the meal field peas and cream corn from Burt's freezer. Gabe always cooked a variety of vegetables that were never wasted. He would cook extra things, and eat leftovers until they were all gone. It's easier cooking a lot of things this way one time, and warming them over during the week, especially if you are by yourself and working all day on farm projects. I also planned to bake Gabe's apple pie. That would be the meal for my start-up project with Old Bessie and Ned.

By the time I had finished breakfast, talked with Burt and to some other curious valley folk, and did my shopping, I had been away from the farm over three hours. There was much to do, which included the dreaded cutting, splitting, and stacking of firewood. I was not looking forward to that backbreaking chore. So, I returned straightaway to the farm.

When I drove up to the house, I quickly noticed that the pile of tree trunks and limbs I had dragged from the forest to the woodpile had been transformed into a neat pile of split firewood. There were two different sizes, as one pile was fireplace width, and the other pile cut in shorter lengths, obviously to be used in Old Bessie. I knew without a doubt there was only one person strong enough to do all that work in such a short time. It was the big guy next door. Ned had no doubt heard me leave in the morning and rushed to get the work done for me.

Along with seeing the condition of his hands, which alerted me there was more to this man than a first impression gives, I was also getting insight into a tender side of him. I had only slightly mentioned I needed to cut wood this morning when I was with him. But it's obvious Ned was listening to every word, and in his own way showed me God was opening a door to his heart that would invite me into it.

With the firewood split and stacked, my day slowed down greatly, and I could enjoy the preparation time needed to cook the meal. I had looked forward to a large, country meal all week, and it was not only for Ned I wanted it to be good. I spent the rest of the day reading and getting a much-needed rest, before starting supper.

I have cooked for several years since Gabe inspired me. So I know my way around the kitchen, at least when cooking the basics such as breakfast and grilling. Preparing a full meal, which means having multiple dishes that finish cooking at the same time, would be a new experience for me. Cooking on Bessie had been previously done under the watchful eye of Gabe. Doing it by myself would also be a new experience. I had his recipes, and making dinner taste even close to his dishes was my target.

To begin with, his fried chicken wasn't prepared by just getting the grease hot, throwing the chicken in the skillet, and cooking it until it was brown. No way! Gabe started his chicken by soaking it in iced, salt water for a few hours. He said it allowed him to cook the chicken slow, and the salty water would make the chicken hold the juices in and keep the grease out. So I started my food prep by soaking the chicken.

While it was soaking, I put the pie together and washed the greens. Not long after this, I gathered firewood and started the fire in the old wood stove. It didn't take long until she was heated up, and the wood settled into a steady, glowing, charcoal base. The Old Girl was ready to feed a couple of hungry men. Before starting my cooking I said a little prayer for help with the cooking project and my evening with Ned. Somehow I recognized this would be a big event in both Ned's and my life, and I wanted it to be special. I didn't know if he would care for my food selection. But I knew one thing for sure, I had better double up on the portions, based on the size of my guest.

An hour or so later, my meal was coming together and close to being finished. About that time, I heard heavy footsteps on the outside porch of the house. I went to the door before Ned had a chance to knock. I opened the door, and the big guy was standing there, acting a little uncomfortable, likely because he hadn't visited with another man in quite a while. I smiled as big as possible and said, "Welcome, neighbor! Come on into this house," while extending my hand for a handshake with Ned. I realized I was sounding more like Gabe with the way he always greeted me. That was a good thing.

He looked at me and smiled. He shifted the guitar he was holding into his left hand, and grasped mine with the other. His hand wrapped around mine like he was holding a child's hand. He could have crushed my hand, but instead gave a firm, but gentle grip.

"Am I on time?" Ned asked.

"Just right," I replied. "Come into the kitchen, and let me finish up our supper. I won't be too much longer, and you can talk to me while I do it."

I led Ned into the kitchen, and pulled a chair over to him. When he sat down, a memory of similar events came to my mind as I thought how Gabe had made me feel so comfortable the first time I met him. I even sat in the same chair and in the same spot of the room Ned was setting in. I had a good mentor with Gabe, and I felt comfortable. He had a knack for making all people feel appreciated and welcomed. I had learned first-hand the truth of being treated in a way one would want a loved one, a friend, or even yourself to be treated. My plan was simple. I would treat Ned like Gabe had treated me, and allow it to take its course.

I handed Ned a large glass of iced sweet-tea, with lemon and mint. He took the mint out and looked for a place to throw it away. I made a mental note, "Don't move too fast with fancy food adornments. Ned probably thinks I put grass in his tea."

"Don't like mint in your tea, Ned?" I asked with a smile.

"Say what?" Ned responded. He didn't have a clue about the mint or my question, so I just let it pass.

"Let me whip up some cornbread, and start it baking. While it's baking, we'll go to the porch and chat until it's done. Everything else is ready."

I busily finished the cornbread batter and put it the oven. Ned and I then went to the front porch and sat in the rocking chairs while chatting rather awkwardly at first. Thank goodness the cornbread finished baking before we ran out of questions by me, and quick responses by Ned. Back in the kitchen, I served Ned's plate from the stove and gave him big portions of everything. When I placed the plate before him, he looked back at me and I asked, "Mind if I pray for the meal?" Ned nodded it was okay.

It was a surreal moment as we bowed our heads. I remembered how Gabe had prayed with me in a similar fashion over our first meal together. He was so relaxed, I innately knew he was not praying for my benefit like many times it is done. No! Gabe poured his heart out before me, for it was a normal thing for him. His example encouraged me to do the same with Ned.

Without hesitation, I grasped Ned's big hand he had placed on the table, and thanked the Lord for the meal and my new friend. I thanked God that he had been a protector of the farm while it was unoccupied. I also acknowledged some kind person had served me greatly by cutting the firewood that morning, and said I suspected it was Ned.

Little by little my prayer poured over into my love for Gabe and his legacy. Tonight especially, because of Gabe's recipes, cooking on Old Bessie, and an opportunity to serve someone as I had been served, I was greatly blessed. Before it went on too long, I ended the prayer. But, it set the mood for the rest of the meal, for Ned and I discussed various meals that could be cooked on the old stove.

It was delightful to hear Ned speak of his old wood stove in an affectionate way, as well, for he too had one similar to Old Bessie. Gabe had also helped him learn to cook new recipes on it. Since he had been cooking on it for 20 years, he was well versed in techniques and recipes of his own. This little conversation about wood stoves gave us common ground, and we quickly moved from an awkward, strained conversation to a truly enjoyable interaction. I was beginning to understand the perceived "Bigfoot" who sat at my table just might be a Renaissance Man in disguise.

I looked forward to what was next, for the guitar Ned brought with him was a vintage Martin made before World War II. It was a beautiful instrument, created at a time when craftsmen sought to optimize the natural acoustics that came from a special made instrument. The electric amp covers a lot of flaws and lack of quality workmanship with many of today's guitars. However, with a guitar such as Ned's, if the right person played it, it could not be matched in sound. I looked forward to what Ned would do with it. The meal wasn't too shabby, either, and I took notice that Ned ate everything set before him. Whether it was good, or he was just hungry, I don't know. But, there were no leftovers.

After the meal, and the washing and putting away of the dishes, we settled back into the rocking chairs on the front porch. Whippoorwills were singing back and forth to each other. Other night sounds also kicked in, and a chorus of insects, birds and frogs sang their "welcome to the farm" songs.

Not waiting for a formal start, I pulled out my harmonica and Ned his guitar. For a warm-up, I played a quick run on the harmonica, giving my best Raw Bones Blues. Ned concentrated on tuning the Martin. I launched into some riffs, thinking I would impress my new friend. He courteously accompanied my efforts by providing rhythm bed on the strings of the old guitar. I could tell he knew rhythm guitar by the way he easily picked up on anything I played.

When I had reached my limit, both in breath and ability, Ned took over the lead. He began to move his left hand effortlessly up and down the neck of his instrument. His long fingers allowed him to create complicated chords I had never seen or heard before, even by some of the best guitar players. His big left hand bridged the neck with little effort, and the flexibility and dexterity in his fingers easily produced any clear note he was calling for. His right hand strummed, picked and coordinated flawlessly while his left hand moved up an down the neck of the guitar.

He ran through a number of songs I recognized as having their roots in the Mississippi Delta. I had heard some of the tunes on vintage blues records. However, I hadn't a clue where some of the others came from, for to my knowledge they were never recorded. They had the simple sounds of Delta Blues, but his improvisation created a new sound, which was his own. Spellbound, I listened and watched his mastery of the guitar. I slowly put my harmonica in my pocket, for I was embarrassingly out of my league. I was watching a master.

Before long, Ned surprised me even more by busting out a few lyrics that accompanied his brilliance on the guitar. His baritone voice was rich, clear and unrestrained. His voice's resonance actually caused loose windowpanes in the house to vibrate! I was in awe. When I saw his hands on our first meeting, I had suspected there was more to the big man than just being a woodcutter. However, I had no idea this night I would be in the presence of genius.

Ned played as if I were not present. His eyes closed and he appeared as if he were in pain. Then it dawned on me. Ned was "feeling" the blues while he sang, for most of the old blues songs were written out of pain, or loss, or coping with something tragic. I could tell he understood on a deep, emotional level the predomi-nant theme of the blues ... *that of being alone.* He was either singing the songs as they were written, or they were written about his life, and he was connecting. I suspected it was the latter. After a while, Ned took a break and drank some of his tea.

I had to ask, "Ned, just how long have you been playing the guitar?"

"About five years now," he replied, "ever since Gabe gave it to me and showed me a few chords. He said his hands had too much arthritis in them, and he couldn't play anymore. When I picked it up and started to play, it came pretty natural. He said somethin' about being gifted, or somethin' like that. Gabe also gave me an old record player with a bunch of 78 speed records. I learned most of my songs from listening to them, and some Gabe taught me."

When Ned spoke of Gabe's experience with music, I had forgotten about his "before Christ" days in Chicago and St Louis. Gabe had previously told me he had run with some pretty wild musicians who had moved up from the Mississippi Delta. He had been with them a couple of years before volunteering with the Army and being sent to England. I had no idea he had actually learned to play the blues, and he knew some of the Fathers of the Delta Blues culture. But, I could also see why Gabe had passed a very special musical instrument along to Ned, for I had never seen such artistry before.

No doubt, Ned was a musical genius. But, he was also an enigma to me. Ned had no social skills or table manners, and he wouldn't look me straight in the eye most of the time. He was painfully shy and well aware he didn't fit in with most people. As brilliant as he was on the guitar, he was equally inept in meaningful interaction with another person. However, I must say I was pleased by our start. I only wish Aunt Mattie and Gabe could have seen what went on that night. They would also have been pleased.

It was getting late. Ned likely would have stayed on the porch all night, for he was relationally starved. I said something about needing to get my rest for a big workday tomorrow, and he caught the hint. We mentioned getting together the next night for another jam session. With that he left, and I headed for bed.

As I lay in bed before dropping off to sleep, I began to review the events of the day and my time with Ned. I could not help but realize God had both prepared the way for our time together, and the way we jelled in our relationship.

Before going into this day, I had felt a deep challenge, wondering if I were the right guy to meet Ned's special needs. I only had the impressions of others to prepare me for our time, as well as my own visual impression, which frightened me at first. The impressions I got from other people saw him in a sense, retarded and unreachable, even dangerous. My initial impression looked at him similarly.

However, with my personal time with Ned, I began to see him differently and lose my fear. As big and as imposing as he was, there was a lot of immaturity and lack of social development that made him act uncomfortable and distant. He wasn't retarded or mentally challenged, for the truth is, he was bright and self-educated, to a degree. No. A better description would be to describe him as a canvas with a very vague outline of a man painted on it, waiting for the right shades and colors to be drawn in. Ned was an uncompleted picture.

I was starting to understand God had dispatched me to join Him in filling in the colors that would bring the man out. Ned had simply not developed because of isolation, and I was chosen to be his mentor in leading him toward social, emotional and spiritual maturity.

I sighed heavily and prayed,

> "Lord, am I ready for this task? Do I have the wisdom needed for, and Your blessing on, this endeavor? If not, I will hurt Ned beyond what has already been done to him. Father, I know of no other plan than to be his friend and help him on his journey of getting to know You. It is only

You Who can transform a man in such need as Ned, not I. It has to be You, Lord. I can only point the way to You, and travel the road with him. I will do this. But Lord, it must be You Who will form him into the man You want him to be."

As I grew sleepy, and just before I dropped off, I heard clear words spoken to my heart that answered my request, and put me to sleep with the encouragement I needed:

"That is all you need do, My child. I will do the rest."

In His gracious way, God was teaching me the Secret of *Divine Dependency*, which is essential if we want to experience what God can accomplish.

CHAPTER SEVEN

The Secret of
Divine Interruption

I awoke with an excitement to press on with mentoring my young neighbor. I could hardly sleep as I thought of different things I wanted to introduce him to. I must say, I went to bed concerned about my part, but woke up with a confidence that things were about to happen for Ned, *and I was the guy to make it so.*

It amazes me sometimes to see how easily I can shift from one position to another, and fall into a trap thinking I can get it done without God's help. Actually, I think it is a basic flaw in the nature of all mankind that we want to accomplish things for God without His help. If we could, we would. But, it will not take long to see our plans cannot succeed without His help, through a process requiring a supernatural intervention. I was headed in the wrong direction, and the Lord had to remind me this was His project, not mine.

It started off innocent enough, as I made plans to take Ned on a little road trip. I planned to load him up in my truck, take him to the nearest large town, and show him the way the rest of the world lives. I was certain he had not been far away from his home his entire life, and it would be a great adventure for him. I wanted to get him a tape recorder, and let him hear songs from various artists, for I wanted to expose him to musical sounds and styles that had developed since the blues of the 30's and 40's.

I drove over to his cabin and saw him working on the old truck. He told me he was taking the water pump and fan belt off in order to get replacements. I asked him if he would drive with me to town, and we could also pick up his parts. He was a little reluctant at first, but gave in to my urging. He washed his hands, put his John Deere baseball cap on his head, and joined me in the truck. Conversation was as it was the night before in that it was still awkward, with me doing most of the talking. I tried to draw him out, but he was so unsure of himself, I could see I needed patience until he became comfortable with me. I could also tell he was concerned about going somewhere unfamiliar to him.

When we first drove into the medium-sized city, Ned's eyes showed his amazement at the number of cars and people flowing around him. I thought it best to ease him into city life with a cone of ice cream, knowing the big guy has a sweet tooth. We stayed in the car, and I drove up to a drive-in window. I ordered a double dip of chocolate ice cream for us, and observed the young woman who served us couldn't take her eyes off Ned. His matted hair and beard, and his size must have been a shock to her, as she ran off from the window to tell her friends to look at Ned. The cone of ice cream was delivered, and Ned busied himself with eating it, while ignoring the gawkers who were watching him. I quickly pulled away from the window, and ate my cone with Ned. It wasn't a pretty sight watching the cream collecting on his beard. But, he thoroughly enjoyed it.

We went next to an auto-parts store, and quickly purchased the truck parts. Ned offered minimal words, by laying the parts on the counter and allowing the clerk to figure out what was needed. We were finally ready for my surprise, as I drove Ned to a music store. I was excited about how Ned would react to the different sounds and styles of music. They had earphones that would allow him to listen to various artists. My plan was to let him hear rock, jazz, classical, and some of the new praise and worship music available. But, it would require Ned going into the music store with me. I was becoming uneasy about this, based on the shock I saw on the ice cream attendant's face.

When we pulled up to the front of the store and parked the truck, I looked at Ned and said, "Ned, I have a great treat for you. I want you to listen to some great songs that have developed since the records you have were produced. I think you will enjoy them. Will you come into the store with me?"

Ned looked surprised, and even happy at first. But, he then looked at the people in the store, hung his head down, and shook his head that he would not go with me.

I said, "Ned, are you afraid of the people?"

Ned bent his head down and said, "They all make fun of me."

In retrospect, I now see that I, the man *who would make things happen for Ned*, was more concerned about my getting him into the store, than to understand what he was going through emotionally at the time. I didn't know his history with people, or his bad experiences. Therefore, in my ignorance I assured him he would not be made fun of, and the people were there to buy music. I stated with assurance that he should come with me, for everything would be all right. How wrong I would be proven to be in this assumption, as Ned trusted my words of assurance and followed me into the store, only to be let down by the one person he was beginning to trust.

Basically, people can be cruel to those who are different, and who seem awkwardly out of place, especially if these people lack maturity themselves. When Ned walked through the front door, all eyes turned to the backwoods, larger-than-average, man. He was not pressed and steamed cleaned in appearance, like the other people. They wore slacks, loafers and button-down collared shirts. Ned wore overalls and brogan boots, with something clinging to the soles. I saw in their faces the same look I had seen on the ice cream girl, followed by an uneasy feeling in my stomach. I maneuvered Ned to the back, thinking the eyes would leave us. They didn't. They continued to follow Ned, with a few snickers from some teenagers. Ned saw their stares, and picked up on the attention he was getting.

I quickly put a tape in Ned's hands, and put earphones on him so he could hear the music. This little move distracted him for a while, as he listened intently to several styles of music. I thought it might ease his embarrassment. It worked for about an hour, as I changed the tapes and let him listen to different kinds of music.

However, the walkway between shelves of music tapes was rather close for any of us, much less for Ned. The store had crammed its merchandise into every space available. When Ned removed the earphones, the cord passed over some loose tapes on the table, and pulled them toward the floor. Ned tried to catch the tapes and protect them, but his sudden movement caused him to back against a stand of tapes on display in the tightly packed space. With a loud noise, the merchandise began to spill over backwards, while Ned attempted to save it. The whole pile landed in a heap. Almost spontaneously, everyone erupted in laughter at Ned's humiliated expression.

How many times would a similar situation occur with a "normal" person, and the only thing happen be a helpful question, "Are you alright?" Ned was given no such courtesy. This is the burden someone who is "different" has to carry each day of his or her life. And if he or she is emotionally or socially immature, the response is more painful than most people can imagine. Such was the case with Ned.

When Ned heard the laughter, he quickly left the building, with louder laughter following after him. After asking the clerk if I need to pay for any damage and was told I didn't, I quickly followed Ned out the door. He was nowhere in sight. I walked around the building, but couldn't find him. I didn't want to shout his name and bring more attention to him. Therefore, I got in the truck, and rode around for about two hours until I found him on the highway headed out of town. Ned had intended to walk the 20 miles back to his house. This was how desperate he was to run back into his secure world.

"Ned," I spoke as I pulled up next to him in my truck, "Will you get in the truck so we can go back home?" Ned never looked at me, and continued to walk toward his home. I understood he blamed me, for I told him nothing bad would happen, and people wouldn't make fun of him.

I caught up with his fast walk and pleaded, "Ned, please get in the truck. I am terribly sorry for what happened back there. They were wrong for laughing at you." He just kept walking.

Finally, I got him to listen when I said, "Ned, I was wrong. You told me people were cruel to you, and I didn't listen to you. There have been times people have also been cruel to me, and I know how it hurts. Will you please ride with me, and let me tell you how you can feel better?"

It came to me that he was dealing with the ridicule as a child would deal with it. I had to look at Ned, the imposing man he was, as a very large child instead. My tactics got him back in the truck, so that I could at least drive him back home. However, he looked out the window the whole time, and never reacted to any word or question I brought up. I dropped him off at his cabin, and he never looked back when he left my truck.

As I returned to the farm, the sickening feeling in my stomach came back as I realized I might have caused irreparable damage to Ned and our relationship. I cried out,

> "Lord, what have I done to this man? How can I recover his fledgling trust in me?"

No voice or comfort to my heart was heard from the Lord, so I drove slowly back to the farm. As I entered the dirt drive to the house, my heart was cheered at the sight of my wife's car. If there was ever a time I needed the comfort of another person and especially her, it was now. When I entered the house, she gave me a big kiss and hug while at the same time seeing the condition of my countenance.

"I thought I would give you a big surprise and drive up to the farm a day early. Instead of joy, I see this sorrow in you." She then placed my face between her hands, looked me square in the eyes, and asked. "What has happened to you today?"

We went to the porch, sat in the rocking chairs, and I gave her a detailed account of my time with Ned, and how it finished so badly. She was able to sympathize with the disappointment I felt for Ned, as well with the way I felt about my role in the process. She was quiet and offered no opinion while I spoke, for she wanted to get a full appraisal before speaking. This is typical of the wise woman she is.

Finally, she asked, "Hon, I followed with you closely up until last night, and it sounded as if God were leading you step-by-step with taking you to Ned, and opening his heart to you. To this point it sounded as if a mysterious process were unfolding before you, and God was completely in control of it all. But this morning, I sensed a change and you got away from God's agenda, and started to make up your own. Is this a possibility?"

I thought on her question and realized I was so astounded with Ned's musical abilities the night before, it became a mission of mine to help him develop in an area I thought would enhance his self-worth. It seemed like a good plan. But I didn't realize how wounded, and even damaged he was because of his experiences from the ridicule he had received from people. Good plan, but wrong plan. It was apparent to me that God had provided a *Divine Interruption* to my plans, and I had no other answer but be totally honest with Dottie.

"No, it's not just a possibility, for it's the truth of what happened," I answered. "I can see I had a good plan, made with a good heart, but I could not see what would happen today. If I had been more careful to pray and seek God's wisdom about my next steps, and be patient, then I believe this afternoon's experience would have been avoided. The question is, can I recover from this with Ned, or does that do it for us?

My wife responded, "Haven't you told me many times our Lord is a God of second chances? Haven't you seen Him help you time and time again when you humbled yourself, asked for His forgiveness, and returned to His plan? Don't you think God is able to overcome any obstacle He has to deal with, as He goes after Ned, even if it is you? Isn't getting back to God's agenda is as simple as getting back to your friendship with Jesus? He desires it, you need it, and He is waiting for you to come to Him. So, let's you and me pray, and wait and watch what God does with Ned and you. It will become obvious if there is an action you must take, or to simply react to what God does with Ned. You will know, for you are asking Him to show you what to do next."

The wisdom and encouragement she blessed me with that night released me from my guilt and reminded me of how incomplete I would be without her. So much of my spiritual journey has been traveled on a narrow path, which mostly included only Jesus and me. However, it has been the people God has given to me who have been used by Him to keep me on the right path. Helpmate? Life mate? Soul mate? Those are words that come pretty close to what I've observed about my relationship with my wife.

As I was thinking about my relationship with this dear woman, I felt God speak to my heart telling me she would become a vital extension of God's love to Ned. I realized He was waiting for her before I should have made the next step. It made sense, since Ned never had a mother figure in his life. I could see how God's plan would require an essential feminine touch to it in order to make it come together for all of us. This thought comforted me.

With joy and relief, I pulled her close to me in a firm embrace and stated, "You are indeed my 'Proverbs 31' woman. You've got a little bit of an attitude, you have? But, you are indeed the real thing!"

We both laughed, and enjoyed the rest of the night of being together. We stayed on the porch until late, and prayed as she had suggested. She went to bed, but I had a little more business to take care of with God, before going to sleep.

I walked off the porch stairs and looked in the direction of Ned's cabin while lifting one hand in the direction of the cabin, and one to the sky, and prayed,

> *"Lord, I see how independent I was in trying to reach Ned in my own wisdom and strength. I am sorry I was so quick to forget this is Your inspired plan in the first place, not mine. I am dependent on You, and need You more so, since I went off unaware and unprepared for what would happen. I ask You to bless Ned as he sleeps tonight. I ask You to work in his heart, as well mine, as You unfold Your plan for reaching him. I don't even know what it will look like. I don't know the man you can make of him because he's been through so much neglect and hurt. He is a wounded child walking around in a man's body. Lord, thank You for giving me my helpmate to join me in this endeavor. She has comforted me, and I believe You will use her to bring comfort to Ned, as well. Father, I trust You, and release this to You. In Jesus' Holy Name I ask these things."*

As I walked back to the farmhouse, I heard these words spoken to my heart,

> *"Follow My lead."*

With assurance, I released my concerns as I realized I was again following my King, rather than trying to lead Him. We were back in His plan, and I was assured all things would work for good. I had made a mistake with my independence. But, God's *Divine Interruption* provided the necessary leadership I needed to get me back to His plan. He provides an interruption in such critical times as this, if we will listen to Him, and turn from our independent ways. I felt better about things, and could rest with the assurance that everything would turn out as He desired.

CHAPTER EIGHT

The Secret of
God's Plan Above All Plans

A few days went by as Dottie and I worked around the farm. There was a lot to do, so we didn't even leave the place. No word from Ned, and when I thought about him being over at his place by himself resenting that I pushed him to go in the music store, I had a sinking feeling in my stomach.

I prayed,

> *"Lord, I want to be part of Your plan and I am waiting for You to show me what it is. But, I feel that I need to do something, because I can't get him off my mind. I think Dottie will play a part, but we've got to make contact with him again. Will You show us how?"*

After my prayer, I went to the truck that hadn't been used in several days, because I wanted to move it inside the barn. I noticed the passenger side door wasn't closed tight from when Ned quickly exited. I looked to see if something was blocking it from shutting, and I saw the cause. There, in its bag from the auto parts store, was the water pump and fan belt Ned had purchased. I looked at the items, and then looked up with excitement to give thanks, for I knew immediately God had given me a reason to go pay Ned a visit.

I ran into the house to tell Dottie. As soon as I entered, a wonderful smell of cookies baking in the oven met my nostrils. I told her I was driving over to Ned's cabin because I felt God had given me a way to make contact again. Not saying anything, she handed me a plate of hot cookies and said, "I understand Ned has a sweet tooth. Tell him there are more of these for him if he will come and play his guitar for me."

After giving her a big hug and kiss, I took the cookies and drove immediately over to Ned's place. When I drove up to his cabin, I saw his truck with the hood up and tools still where they were when I convinced him to go to town with me. No sign of him, but that didn't mean he wasn't there. He could be in the house hiding. But he had likely walked to his next job.

I said to myself, "Ned, you might have a little too much pride. You would rather walk to work than come to our house and get your parts."

I left Dottie's cookies on the porch with a note saying exactly what she asked me to tell Ned. I also took the bag of parts over to the truck, and put them next to the tools. As I walked away to go back to my truck, a picture of my stack of split firewood came to mind. I paused, thought about it, and turned back to Ned's truck while saying to myself, "One good deed deserves one in return."

I rolled up my sleeves, grabbed Ned's tools, and replaced the water pump and fan belt. It took only about an hour. I looked in the truck and the keys were in the ignition, so I poured antifreeze in the radiator, and allowed it to circulate while the truck was running. Satisfied that everything was working properly, I shut the hood, took his tools and the replaced parts to the front porch, and placed them by the cookies so he would be able to see the work had been completed on the truck. I only wish I could have done it anonymously the way he did with my firewood. But maybe he needed to know it was me, for he would at least have a reason to respond. I drove directly home and resumed my chores.

After dinner Dottie and I were sitting on the porch discussing the children and grandchildren, which is a common subject for us. I was saying something to her when she interrupted me, "He is big isn't he? I'd better get some pie to go with those cookies."

I turned around and looked in the direction she was looking. Emerging from the woods between his place and ours, was Ned carrying his guitar. He walked shyly to the porch. I tried hard to not be obviously excited, so I just said, "Hey Ned, come for a visit?"

By that time Ned had stepped on the porch and sat down as Dottie came out with a plate of cookies, a slice of pie, and a glass of milk. She spoke quickly, "Hi, Ned, I am so glad to meet you. I've heard some great things about your singing and playing a guitar. By the way, here's my promise in return to hear you," as she handed him the plate of cookies and pie.

I had to admire the way she put Ned at ease. The cookies and pie brought a broad smile to his face. She was also able to engage him in conversation and get him to talk, which was no easy task for me. There was something about the missing feminine ingredient I now could see was needed. It would be a family project to win and secure a friendship with Ned, for he was the most wounded and shy individual I had ever met. I could now see *The Secret of God's Plan* now unfolding in front of me. I felt secure all the parts were in motion because of Dottie's contribution. I would follow the flow, and watch how God would move next.

When Ned finished his dessert, he started to tune his guitar and looked at me while asking, "You joinin' me?"

"Had the harmonica in my pocket ready to go," I answered.

This time Ned led out and I did my best to follow him. I felt like a small pony running full speed next to a thoroughbred horse that was just loping along at one fourth of his top speed, so the pony could keep up with him. Ned was gracious with his pace, but I realized I was holding him back, and said, "You take it from here."

Ned nodded his head, and moved smoothly into chords and songs he had shown me a few days before. I watched my wife's lower jaw literally drop from amazement as she watched Ned. She could see for herself the musical genius of the shy, huge, man I had spoken about, and who was now sitting on our porch. After his opening run, Ned then played a new song. It was a beautiful blend of different musical genre ranging from classical, to jazz, to rock.

I asked him, "Ned, I've never heard this music before, but it sounds somewhat familiar. Where did it come from?"

"I wrote it after we got back from town," he responded. "A lot of those songs I heard started to mix together in my mind, so when that happens, I just sit down and pick it out on the guitar."

"Ned," I said while trying to contain myself, "We were in the music store for only an hour, and you only listened to those songs one time. How could you remember them so quickly?"

"I don't know," he responded. "It just comes easy for me."

Dottie moved from her chair and came near to Ned. She took his big hand, while looking at him closely, and then she said, "Ned, you are very, very special. God has created a very precious man when He created you. You can do things with music only a few people in history could do. Do you understand how special you are to God?"

Ned began to look away from her, hoping to avoid eye contact, but she would not let him go into his shell. She moved her eyes and face with his, so he would have to look her in the eyes. He was forced to embrace her eyes with his.

As she intently gazed into his eyes Dottie asked, "Can I teach you another song I believe will mean a lot to you, for it sure means a lot to me?"

Without waiting for permission, she sang "Amazing Grace" with her beautiful voice. She sang all the stanzas, and when she finished, she said, "Ned, the words of that song were written by a man who had two lives. One life was before he came to know Jesus, and the other was after he found the amazing grace God gave to him through Jesus. Did you hear words that told you what his old life was like, and what his new life became?"

Ned nodded and responded, "He said he had been lost and was found, had been blind, but now he could see. He said he was afraid, but his fears had been taken away, that he had been in danger, but grace had got him through it. Then he said somethin' at the end of the song about a place he will one day be, that even 10,000 years bein' there will only be the start."

Now it was my time to drop my jaw, because Ned had quickly dissected the heart of a song that takes most of us years to understand the truths Newton was reflecting from his life. Like the blues he could grasp so easily because of his own struggles with life, he had heard the soul of the song, and could relate to the inner struggle that went on in Newton's life. Obviously, he didn't know what those struggles were, so Dottie kept her connection with him by asking, "Ned, would you like me to tell you the story of the man who wrote that song and what those words meant to him, and to me as well?"

When Ned nodded he did, she then told the story of John Newton's life. She started Newton's story with him losing his family at an early age, and pointed out that in a way it was similar to the way Ned had lost his family. She then went on to tell of Newton's life at sea, starting when he was only a teen, and how he was often misunderstood, and got into trouble a lot. She then related it to him being misunderstood in the music store. She told of how Newton had jumped ship, and became a deserter from the Navy. After his capture and release, he became a servant for a brutal plantation owner in West Africa where he was abused. She shared how he then escaped, was rescued by a passing slave ship, and eventually became the captain of a slave ship that made numerous crossings of the Atlantic Ocean with many slaves dying on the way. She led Ned through Newton's life from that point up to a life-changing event when he faced a powerful storm he had to steer his ship through. It was during that storm he gave his life to Jesus.

Dottie told Ned that Newton described himself as having lived a "degrading life of debauchery" before his conversion, and explained to him what the phrase meant. She said Newton came to conclude his life was bound for hell, unless he accepted the grace God extended him through Jesus. As a wrap-up, she gave a brief biography of Newton's life after he received Christ, and his work to abolish the slave trade England sponsored. She also explained it was during this time Newton penned the words to Amazing Grace based on his own life story.

I watched the drama unfold before me, as Ned's eyes were transfixed on Dottie. He barely blinked his eyes as she told Newton's story, and how it connected to the song Dottie had just taught him. I felt he could "see" the story of Newton in his mind's eye, and it caused him to relate even more deeply with the truths in the song. After my wife finished, Ned excused himself with saying only, "Appreciate it," and "Gotta go."

When Ned left, we just stared at each other not knowing what to say next. I led out by asking, "What do you think? Did we offend him or scare him away?"

She answered, "He's very, very special, but it will take a lot of prayer and patience to reach him. That poor boy is so deeply wounded, and suspicious because of isolation and bad experiences with people, it will take a divine work of God to reach him."

Not waiting, I grasped Dottie's hand and offered up a request that God would allow the words spoken to Ned to sink deeply into his heart. I sensed what was needed was for Ned to take the next step, and come back to us. We had to allow the Holy Spirit time to work in his heart. Ned had not allowed anyone into his life to this point, except for Gabe through music, and Aunt Mattie with her occasional cakes.

I felt he was like a wild animal that wanted to come close, but when doing so, would bolt with the slightest provocation. If he sensed we had a hidden agenda other than just being friends, he would run away, and never return. Truly, Dottie and I didn't know what to do next except wait for God and Ned to connect, and be available for him. As it turns out, this was the most important thing we could have done.

As Dottie finished her work in the kitchen, I took my customary prayer walk down our little driveway to the road.

> *"Lord, I ask You to walk us through the next steps as to how to serve Ned. We need Your work in his life, as well ours, so we can reach him. We place ourselves before You as a living sacrifice, and submit to Your leadership. I only ask Your work to precede everything we are invited to be part of, and we are following Your plans and not our own."*

I was again aware I was beginning to understand the *Secret of God's Plan* above mine, the way I should have all along. I felt comfort in knowing the patience Dottie and I were committed to maintaining as we waited for Ned to respond, was inspired by God. I know there are different opinions about how believers should serve the Lord in reaching the lost. Some are more aggressive than others. However, I have discovered a strong fervor to serve Him, can often times cause us to work for God, rather than with Him. Some "soul winning" efforts can look at saving a lost soul like bagging a trophy elk.

The truth is, no Christian converts another person. We only lead someone to the Source where that person must choose to accept the Hand of Grace that is extended to him or her. Conversion is between the Holy Spirit and the man or woman. We simply work with God to point the way to Him. Yes, God may use us to clearly explain the Good News of the salvation He offers. But, our most involved contribution as a Christian begins in the next stage of a new convert's life, as we love, nurture, and prepare him for a new life with Christ. God's family becomes His discipleship tool, as long as we operate from His inspiration and perspective.

After my prayer walk, I returned to the house, and joined Dottie who was already asleep in bed.

CHAPTER NINE

The Secret of
God's Compelling Grace

I t was several days before Ned returned. During that time, Dottie and I continued to pray for him and take care of the chores that come with a farm. We had just finished dinner and were sitting on the front porch when the big man emerged from the woods and approached the farmhouse. He had his guitar in hand.

Dottie went into the house for cookies while he made his way on the path to our porch. When he approached, I raised a hand and declared, "Howdy, neighbor!"

"Thought I would drop by if you and Miss Dottie don't mind." Ned said.

"Glad you did," I replied. "I wondered if you smelled Dottie's cookies being baked today?"

Then I thought that maybe I ought not have mentioned the cookies, for I saw an embarrassed look on Ned's face. I think he really did smell them, and was drawn to the wonderful aroma. "So what?" I thought. "God lures us to Him in many ways. Why not cookies?"

"Well, uh ... I guess ...," Ned stammered.

Quickly interrupting, I said with a smile, "Man, I'm glad you're here! I can't eat all those cookies by myself. You saved me some embarrassment. Dottie takes it real personal when I don't clean the plate."

About that time, Dottie came through the door with a plate of freshly baked cookies along with three cups of hot coffee while declaring, "Cookies and coffee for music, anyone?" The stage was set.

After some small talk, and when all the cookies were finished, Ned opened his guitar case and tuned the Martin. Then he looked at Dottie and asked, "I hope you don't mind I changed a few things with your song?"

Then he launched into a breathtaking run of chords that intertwined the familiar melody of "Amazing Grace" with a composition I had never heard before. A build-up of rhythm and chords provided a foretaste to the lyrics he would sing. When his preamble was complete, Ned began to sing the lyrics to his song. In an easy, yet deeply connected way, he sang every word without missing a one. He had heard it only one time, and yet it had fastened in his memory.

Toward the end of "Amazing Grace," Ned subtly transitioned into new lyrics and rhythm. It was a creative melody played softly behind his words without a strong metrical pattern. "Soft background supporting his words," would describe what he was doing.

Ned sang words Dottie and I knew transitioned from Newton's life to his own. They were a reflection of a life and perspective hidden from all other human beings. In his silent world of isolation, an intelligent man processed life as it was given to him, and one he had been denied. This was a man with only an elementary education and who had trouble speaking directly to anyone. But, with his heart and emotions engaged with his musical genius, his song expressed clearly the answer he had found in God's *Compelling Grace* to him. He sang:

Compelled by Grace

"This man once saw the beauty of the stars, and asked Who formed them.
He asked if there is 'One who sees him, or One Who knows him, or does He even care?'

Then this man heard there's a grace that compels, a grace excels all his faults, but, can this be true?
Can this man be made so clean, by One so good and could wash away all his stains?
Can there be One so good, could love so right, even though this man knows not His name?

Can there be a grace that brings what he's longed for, and a grace that gives him hope?
Can there be a grace that wakes his heart to feelings he never knew, and a grace that shows him the reason why?

Can there be a grace that shows him how incomplete he is, and yet a grace that makes him complete?
Can this be true? Can this be true that one such as this man, can be found and loved by One so good as You?

Can there be more perfect love, than this Man would die for me?
This Man died for me!
Now, this Man Jesus gives His grace,
and He gives His grace to me!

83

What must I do? What else can I do, but take this grace that longs in me?
What else can I do? What must I do?
I must take this grace that's been shown to me!

Love so amazin', cause grace is so amazin', this man now can see.
It's Him Who's amazin', it's Jesus Who's amazin'
'cause He gave His grace to me!

Life's so amazin', and joy is a-growin', 'cause now I walk with Thee!
Stars now amazin' and nights are a-blazin',
'cause Your grace taught me how to see,
Your grace taught me how to see!"

After Ned finished, Dottie was a puddle of tears. We knew he had declared his faith in Jesus with his song. There was a moment of silence, and then we both rushed to Ned, and all three of us embraced on the porch. Ned was a little reluctant at first, but suddenly he wrapped his big arms around both of us, and pulled us to his body.

Then he began to weep uncontrollably. Long, deep sobs of pain were released from him as we could feel years of frustration and loneliness being reconciled by human bodies touching him, and the love of the King of the Universe reveling in the three of us. We felt Ned's spiritual healing flowing into him with the embodiment of Christ reaching in, through and around all of us.

Yes, Grace made His way to the front porch of Gabe's farmhouse again, and another lost soul had entered God's family. But, something else happened, for he was also given a family who would accept and love him as one of their own. From that day forward, Ned would become our adopted son, and we his parents. Since we only had daughters, he would become the son we never had, and Dottie the mother he never knew. Dottie and I also would become "Mom and Pop" in name to him not long after that night.

Ned had come to a conclusion, and declared it in his song that night. Some would think he saw grace for the first time, and embraced it. But, grace had been reaching to him for many years before that night through the faithful service of Aunt Mattie, and the wise initiations by Gabe.

What Dottie and I saw was the "fruit of the harvest," as he connected something we said and did with his life. In doing so, it finally made sense to him. Both Gabe and Aunt Mattie had planted and sowed years of truths about Jesus and God's plan to reach him. Without the faithful sowing of truth and prayer by these friends, there would have been no reaping. This thought made me understand clearly the truth of what Jesus said, *"One sows and another reaps. I sent you to reap what you haven't worked for. Others have done the hard work and you have reaped the benefits of their labor."*

Dottie and I understood our part in his life would become a marvelous repeat of the relationship I had with Gabe, as a circle would be completed with I, who was once the *Learner* now becoming the *Mentor* to Ned, who was now the new Learner. "What a plan God has for discipling His kids," I thought.

There would be many years required of Dottie and me, with God's help, to overcome Ned's arrested development. We would be with him almost every night we came to the farm, which became more frequent, and for longer periods of time. His old cabin was in bad shape, so we asked him to move in with us and live in the spare room.

We then asked that he transition from being a woodcutter, who was gone most of the day, to become the overseer of our 80-acre farm. I taught him how to farm the land and Dottie home schooled him. We allowed him to keep all the profits produced from the hay, crops and cattle. By this means, he became financially independent, and able to save his money for things he would need. Because he was so smart and eager to learn, Ned was able to move from basic to advanced studies quickly. Eventually, Dottie had him tested, and as a result he was awarded his GED. There was no surprise to us when it was discovered Ned's IQ test also revealed he was a brilliant man.

Of great delight to the three of us was our nightly exploration of the Bible for spiritual truths. Ned became firmly rooted in God's Word which helped him grow is wisdom. Dottie worked on his appearance by removing much of his facial hair, which immediately created a more civilized appearance. She fed him with healthy food, and as a result he lost some unneeded weight.

We didn't realize how strikingly handsome he was until his weight was reduced, his hair was trimmed, his beard was removed, and he was dressed in stylish clothes. Even so, I was concerned about his interaction with the public, for to this point he was rarely with other people. What Dottie and I didn't realize, however, was how God was preparing Ned within himself for that aspect of his life. It took a football game to show me what had been going on by God to prepare him for the public, and to overcome the ridicule that always seemed to come his way.

Ned had never been to a football game, and he loved to listen to any being played on the radio. The football team for the county high school he followed would be playing in a championship game, so Dottie suggested I take him to it. It had been over two years, but I was still reeling from the music store incident, and wasn't sure he was ready to meet the public again. But, I agreed, and he did, too. Ned was cleaned up, and looked like a changed man. To some, he would be unrecognizable as the old man who was ridiculed in that music store the year before. However, for others, especially some teenagers, they would recognize the "strange man," even though he had changed in appearance. Such was the case at the ballgame.

The stadium was packed that night, and we had to sit below the student section. Ned and I were enjoying the game, and the home team was winning. The students above us were having a good time, and we were on the home team side of the stadium. Shortly after the halftime break, the first peanut hit Ned's shoulder. Next came popcorn. Before long, his back became target practice for some of the teenagers a few rows behind us.

I watched Ned, but he didn't flinch, and he acted as if he didn't feel anything hitting him, or notice the laughter going on behind him. I was deeply concerned he would revert back to the child who felt ridiculed growing up, and would react with immature emotions, not to mention the possibility of how dangerous he could be if he wanted. He had been doing so well, and I was concerned with what would happen next. I began to grow angry with the teenagers behind us. "Why did this have to happen, Lord?" I asked as I breathed a silent, angry prayer. It had been a long time since I boiled over with anger, but it was getting ready to erupt, and I felt great justification in letting it go.

Just as I began to stand up from my seat to pay a visit to the teenagers behind us, a big hand fell across my knees and wouldn't allow me to stand. Ned had placed his hand on them. I looked at him, and he continued to calmly watch the game and eat his popcorn, while holding me in my seat.

Without looking directly at me, but speaking to me nonetheless, Ned said, "Pop, you and Mom have been teachin' me from the Bible that all Scripture is inspired by God, and gives us directions for right behavior. Is that right?"

Diverted from my anger, and taken aback by his question, I stammered out the obvious answer, "That's right, Ned. That's exactly what we were saying."

Ned paused and allowed his question and my answer to sink in while he took a drink of soda to wash his popcorn down. Almost changing the subject, but making the connection in the next sentence, he said, "I was readin' a verse from Proverbs the other day. It said, *'Do not answer a fool according to his folly, or you will be like him yourself.'* Now I got to thinkin' about that verse and my life. I remember when I used to act mighty foolish because of the way some people treated me. People laughin' at me always seemed to follow me, and I always reacted the same way as well. Right then I understood what you and Mom were tellin' me about God's Word, and how it would guide me with how to act. I understood that God's Word was preparin' me how to act when something like people laughin' at me came up again."

Ned paused almost if he were finished. But he wasn't. The peanuts and popcorn were still hitting his back. A moment later, he slowly turned his head and looked at me confidently, straight in the eyes, which was starting to happen more frequently with him.

He asked, "Pop, is God speakin' to you and me about those kids back there throwin' things at me? Is He tellin' us not to act like them? Maybe there's somethin' bigger going on here. Maybe God's allowin' this test so it will help me overcome my own foolish behavior. So, let's not you and me be like them. OK?"

Then he smiled, gave me a wink, turned his head and continued to watch the game while saying, "Great game, huh?"

Ned was right. The kids in the back eventually got bored with their prank, and concentrated on the game again. But, if there was ever a time that my heart wanted to leap out of my chest with joy, it was right then. Watching Ned's wisdom unfold before me was enough. But, it was if I could hear God clearly speaking to my own heart and saying,

> "See, my child? I've got Ned in My care. His transformation has begun. Watch what I will do with him from this time on."

That night was only the beginning of an amazing transformation of Ned's life. All the years that were lost in his past life were made up for a hundred fold, as God took Ned by hand and molded him into one of the most outstanding human beings I have ever known. Two years after this night, he continued his formal education at the local community college.

His musical ability was discovered, and he was urged to try out in a talent contest. He sang a song he had written, and won the contest easily. The audience wanted more, and he sang another of his compositions, which astounded all of us. It didn't take long for the discovery of his song writing ability to be made known to the business end of the music industry, as his music was sought constantly by Gospel and Country musicians.

Ned eventually became a wealthy man because of the success of his songs, but he chose to never live away from the valley. He met and fell in love with a beautiful young woman at the college. They married, and she brought more blessings of love and balance to Ned, for she bore him three beautiful children. They bought the property next to his cabin, and built a simple, but comfortable, home for their growing family. Ned then gutted his old cabin and made it into a studio for his writing.

We watched our adopted son and his family grow in every way, and it brought joy to us as we could never have imagined something so amazing happen for Ned. Only God could do such a work in a person's life as He had done with Ned. Indeed, it was God's "Amazing Grace" reaching into Ned's heart, and transforming him inside out, as He is willing to do for all of us.

CHAPTER TEN

The Secret of *Right Standing with God*

I t was during Ned's community college days, while he was gone during the day, that I had more free time. I had not forgotten my interest in getting an answer about how Gabe's farm fed the residents during a particular hard time in the Valley's history. So I began to search for the answer, in earnest. Before, every time I got close to a person who could give me some answers, I seemed to be redirected to another agenda.

I'm not complaining though, for with each redirection, I could see clearly the hand of God being on something that was more important, such as Ned. I am learning that if I want to live in an abiding relationship with my King, then I must hold my personal agenda loosely, and allow Him to override it.

This time, however, I felt this pursuit had God's timing on it, and the story, when understood, would unveil more revelations of how a man, simply by living in his world faithfully with God by daily abiding in Christ, could impact his world in a supernatural, culture-changing way. I call this the Secret of *Right Standing with God*, as it proved to be the case for the people of the valley.

When I last met with Aunt Mattie, I asked her to tell me the story I was looking for about Gabe's farm. However, she declined, and instead, she told me there were some people who could share the total story of that period, and I should talk to them. I was even more intrigued when I heard there was more to the story than what I had already heard about Gabe and the farm.

"You mean, there's more to it than the obvious?" I asked.

"Oh yes," Aunt Mattie replied. "Much more, and when you hear how it all worked together, you will understand how Gabe provided more than just food in a hard time. He led us to God and to freedom, and he showed us how a true Christian should live."

Now, I really wanted some answers. So I asked, "Who are these people that I need to talk to, and where do I find them?"

"His name is Reverend L. Nathan Schumacher, and his wife is Nelda. She's a feisty thing, but as good a sweetheart as you'll find. People in the valley call him 'Pastor Nate.' He is the retired minister of the Lutheran Church here in the valley. We all cherish him because of the great work he did with Gabe in bringing Christ to the valley, and helping us see the evil that was choking the spiritual life out of it. He's been the shepherd of the valley for years."

"Another story," I thought. Every time I explored one part of the valley's history, another story would emerge.

After talking more with Aunt Mattie, I found out that Pastor Nate's and Gabe's story intertwined, and I would have to hear it all if I wanted to truly understand what happened. I now had the time for the pursuit, and was on my hunt like a bird dog. So, I drove to the Lutheran parsonage looking for some answers.

When Pastor Nate retired, the parsonage had been deeded over to him and his wife. Although he no longer served in the pulpit, he continued to shepherd the people of the parish. Therefore, being close to the church physically helped him to respond when needed.

I had already discovered the beautiful Lutheran church, for it was in the center of the valley, and was also an important part of the valley's history. Like so many other settlements in rural America, emigrants from Europe had moved into this valley and created family farms. In our valley, German emigrants had settled the valley. It was understandable that the first common effort of the community of people who lived here was to build a Lutheran church, as it would not only serve as a place of worship and spiritual growth, but also as a community center. These early pioneers were not concerned about separating church from other aspects of life because it was already integrated within the fabric of the community.

In this day and time, we tend toward forgetting this essential part of our country's history and greatness as we try to adjust politically and governmentally in order to adapt to social reformation. As a result, there is great concern by many people that the foundation of this nation is being eroded because we are pushing out of our national fabric the vital link of our community churches to this nation's heart and development. I suppose this is why I seek as much wisdom as I can find from the older generation of Christian men and women, for they helped form this nation, and took it through some difficult periods in its development. There is still much to learn from them, and their great insight needs to be listened to and understood before this generation passes. Sadly, the twilight of their lives is upon them.

I approached the church in my truck, while going up the drive leading to it. While driving in my truck to the church, I was able to see the tall, white, massive steeple from miles away. The steeple is at the front of the church and houses bells that have rung for many years on every Sunday morning, and on holidays. The bells can be heard throughout the valley, giving the people a simple reminder that church is open and awaiting its flock.

The church has a simple, but beautiful, architecture, with tall, arched windows on the front and sides of the church, and white, painted, wood siding from front to back. The craftsmanship is of Old World quality for which the German settlers were well known. A "work of love" is also evident to me by the way the old church stands in the valley, and the way it is maintained. The small parsonage is a short walk from the church, and has the same beautiful, but simple design as the church, with a picket fence surrounding the front yard.

When I first viewed the little cottage, I was immediately captivated by its charm. I didn't have to look long for Pastor Nate, for he was in the front yard on his knees working over his flower garden. As I drove up the driveway to the cottage, Pastor Nate slowly stood up from his work to see who had come for a visit.

"Howdy," I said cheerfully as I got out my truck. "Are you Pastor Nate?"

The old man dropped his hand spade next to the flowerbed, took off his gloves, and cheerfully responded, "It depends on who's asking. If you are a city person, then I'm just Nathan. But, if you're a valley resident, then I'm Pastor Nate. So, which are you?"

"Well, I guess that makes you Pastor Nate to me," I declared, "since I bought the farm down the road, and now come to the valley as often as possible," I declared.

"Oh, I've heard about you," Pastor Nate said as he reached for my hand to shake. "You and Ned have become close friends. Aunt Mattie told me all about it. You are an answer to our prayers. That boy has needed a man friend in his life, and someone who can help bring him out of that tiny world he has been limiting himself to."

"I'm not so sure it hasn't worked both ways for Ned and me," I said. "When I think I'm serving him, I find just being around him generally returns to me a blessing more than I give. He is a very special person."

"It generally works that way. The good we do to others, God Himself comes back and does the same for us," Pastor Nate spoke with kind assurance. "Why don't you come sit for a while, and meet Mrs. Shumacher? I'll ask her to brew some tea, and join us."

"My pleasure, Pastor Nate," I responded.

Pastor Nate left me on the porch to go and wash the dirt off his hands and make his request to his wife. I watched him walk away. He was a small man, spry and quick witted. I would estimate he was in his 80s at the time. But like so many of the other older people of the valley, he didn't show his age, and wouldn't likely be limited much with what he wanted to get done. I was finding so much pleasure in getting to know the older generation of the people in the valley, and the wisdom I gained from them. I could also see Pastor Nate had a shepherd's heart that invited anyone into it. He was made for his calling, and retirement never removed him from his ministry. It only shifted the administrative burden from him, and freed him to serve better. Nate returned with Nelda, his wife, along with hot tea and cookies.

Nelda had the look of a pastor's wife from her generation, in that she was prim and proper in dress and speech. She offered a willing smile to everything Pastor Nate said, and affirmed his strong convictions with her nods. But as God often does, He counterbalanced Pastor Nate's enthusiasm and passion with a gentle grace in his wife that asserted God is on His throne, and all our failures can never undo His love for us. This was a good reminder for a man who didn't see all his work come to yield good fruit, and the temptation to take it personally. But Nelda was also her own woman, and wouldn't hesitate to speak out with confidence. She had a little spark in her words, and I could see she wouldn't back down too easily from her convictions. They were quite the team.

After our introductions and having established some common links, the perceptive Nelda asked me for the real purpose of my visit, which I quickly launched into.

First, I shared my story of getting to know Gabe as a friend and mentor, and eventually coming to purchase his house and land. Next, I shared my heart for using the farm as a place of refuge for people who need to connect to a simple, rural life, and the blessing they receive from it when they visit. I shared about Gabe's funeral, and found out they were in the large crowd of people who attended it. They came to understand my love for Gabe, and how God had used him so greatly to influence me into a deep, intimate relationship with Christ. I shared with them how Burt, at the general store, had intrigued me with his comment about how Gabe's farm was used to feed so many of the valley residents at a particularly hard time in the valley's history, and how Aunt Mattie deepened the intrigue when she told me there was much more to the story than this fact.

I summed it all up by saying simply I wanted to know the *total story*, for there is much that needs to be remembered, and learned, from the past experiences of great people. I considered Gabe to be one of them. Little did I realize at the time, the small man and woman who sat with me on their porch would also play a significant part because of the courage they displayed in their part of the *total story*.

Pastor Nate and Nelda listened intently while rocking in their chairs. Each one took a sip of tea and nibbled on a cookie as they contemplated my reasons for wanting to meet them, and my desire to know the *total story* about Gabe and his impact on the valley. Nate looked at Nelda and spoke gently, "Dear, you have your own perspective that needs to be heard, as well. So, don't let me do all the talking." Nelda nodded that she agreed.

"First off," Pastor Nate began, "let me say we share the same love and admiration for Gabe as you do. But it wasn't always so." This surprised me, a little, that a negative statement about Gabe would begin so soon. But the next statement helped me understand Pastor

Nate was speaking of a negative appraisal of himself and Nelda, rather than of Gabe.

"Nelda and I moved into the valley fresh out of seminary. I was wet behind the ears, and raring to go. I wanted to save the lost and set the captives free from their slavery to sin. But, I hadn't yet come to understand going to church doesn't always mean being a true Christian, or calling oneself a Christian doesn't always mean living like one. It was my first experience with pastoring my own church, and we had a lot to learn."

Nate continued, "I read something that an old Baptist preacher once said, and it pretty well spoke to the issue of what we were facing. He said, 'Rote, Rut, Rot.' In other words when we get into the business of church, and into the culture of church, when we get into the habit of church, and into the traditions of church, we often get into 'rote.' When rote sets in with our Christianity, it leads us into a spiritual 'rut.' And when we get into this spiritual rut, it leads to fruit 'rot' in that we just do not see the great works of God being accomplished in our lives, and in our church. This is what we faced with the congregants who attended the church when we first came to pastor it. They had their ways, and they would not change no matter what I taught, or how I taught it. Before long I began to join them, and simply settled myself to live in a beautiful valley with good people and to not upset them. I provided sermons, and pastored the people the best I could. At least that's how I saw it then."

Nate finished, and looked at Nelda to invite her comments.

"Well," Nelda responded, "you didn't know at the time there was any other way, or at least we thought so. Besides, times were hard, and having a steady job with a church meant a lot to us, and the family we hoped to build. We didn't know at the time we couldn't have children of our own, so we thought we needed to protect Nathan's job foremost. Nathan had worked several jobs, as he put himself through college and seminary. We were excited about living in the country, and in this beautiful valley. We had high goals at first, and thought we just needed time to turn the hearts of the people by preaching about a Christ Who is alive, rather than the historical figure they worshipped. But, we compromised our message, and before long 'Rote, Rut, Rot' set into our lives, as well, as it was already with the congregation. But, not completely, for we still had a glimmer of hope that there was someone out there who lived his life in such a way that every day was a spiritual adventure with God. Actually, he was living in the valley, but we never paid any attention to him, for he didn't fit the model of what we thought he needed to look like."

"Was it because he was a poor, black, uneducated farmer?" I asked, a little condescendingly.

"Yes, mostly, among other things," Nate responded while shaking his head in shameful resignation. "Gabe and his family were unknown, unthought-of, and of course excluded, because they were different from the rest of the valley people. Don't get me wrong. There wasn't any outright bigotry toward them. If so, we would have sniffed it out and made an outright challenge to it. We were too high-minded for that kind of activity. But, the truth is, what was going on with the people around here was a hidden, cultural, prejudice that wouldn't come out in the open, for it lay beneath the surface of our lives. I suspect this was even worse, because it had us all thinking we were ahead of our times in our openness to, and tolerance of, integration issues. We couldn't iden-tify with those hooded hoodlums who burned crosses and hated blacks. So, we felt proudly comfortable with ourselves. But make no mistake in thinking otherwise. We were prejudiced because we pre-judged Gabe and his family, and put them into a stereotypical mold. Even though we had never spoken to them, or spent any time with them, we thought we had them figured out. By the way, please note that I am saying, 'we' as I share this, for Nelda and I were just as guilty as the rest of the people around here."

I understood clearly what Pastor Nate was saying, for I, too, was raised in a home that was proud of the fact we didn't hate or pre-judge anyone because of their color. We were also very critical of the white hate groups that did their evil, and we detested being stereotyped in with them just because we were Southerners. But, the truth is, we had no black friends. There were no black people where we worshipped. In our home, our attitude was the black people had their own lives, their own culture, their own friends, and we had ours. So, we had no connection with understanding their plight, their needs, or their desires as humans. Worst of all, we didn't understand how many things we had in common, for it would have changed our prejudiced views. It was "us and them" in our thinking. Simply put, we didn't see ourselves as prejudiced.

But, like Pastor Nate said about himself and his people, my family and I were also fooling ourselves into a sense of comfortable isolation, and neutral morality, by our cultural prejudice hidden beneath the surface of our lives.

"How did it change?" I asked, as I looked at Pastor Nate.

Not to be left out, Nelda wanted to give her enthusiastic response first, so she answered the question. "I tell you what changed us. It required a courageous man to step out and treat people the way Jesus would, and to live his life out in front of us, as well as do the things we only talk about in church. Gabe and his wife, Katherine, showed us how a Christian should live his and her life for God's glory, and it made us ashamed of ourselves. Gabe didn't preach, and he didn't try to stand out. However, there was something about him that spoke to us about his heart and his view of life. He had more moral authority than anybody around these parts, because he was the real thing!"

Pastor Nate was nodding a strong approval as Nelda spoke.

Nelda continued, "The other thing is we believe God got fed up with the pride and complacent existence we all had around here. We were taking too much for granted. We had steady rain, a good growing climate, and our harvest from the farms was always predictable. Most everyone in this valley, except Gabe and his family, went to this church. But there was no spiritual life or enthusiasm with us. Nate preached his heart out, at first. But, before long, he grew discouraged and settled into just going through the motions. We'd sing all our great Lutheran songs, and we felt real

99

good as a congregation that we were giving a witness to the people of the valley who didn't go to church when they heard us singing. But, it was all rote. It was only habit. We had lost our hearts."

"Gabe taught us a thing or two about one of our great songs, didn't he?" Nate said, as he winked at Nelda. She smiled and nodded, as they shared their secret.

"Oh, yeah? Tell me about it," I asked.

"Well, I guess this is where the total story that Aunt Mattie was talking about starts to come together. So, why don't I lay out the whole story to you, before I answer that question?" Nate asked.

I was on the edge of my seat as I nodded enthusiastically that I wanted to hear the story. I had wanted to hear this story since Burt first stirred my thoughts about it when I first met him. Now I had some more bait dangled before me with their comments about a song.

"To begin with, I must share with you where Nelda and I were at the time. We had been pastoring the church for over fifteen years. The previous pastor had died after serving the church over 30 years. Like I said before, we were called to pastor the church soon after I finished seminary. I was 30 years old when we moved here. I was becoming very disappointed in my calling, our future, and myself as the pastor of this church. The congregation was casual, at best, in their faith, and their expression of it. They had no heart for missions or evangelism. They were not concerned for each other, and especially anyone outside of the church. They were simply selfish in most things as evidenced by their lack of support for the mission of the church. In fact, there were many times we couldn't even pay our bills at the church, and I had to take in an extra job to make ends meet. The people were all comfortable, self centered, and satisfied with their lukewarm existence. I couldn't shake them out of it, and would have settled in with them, if God hadn't made things uncomfortable for Nelda and me."

Pastor Nate continued. "I was ready to leave the ministry and move out of the valley, for I had had enough. I didn't want anything more to do with the people or the job. When I told Nelda what I was thinking, she challenged me by asking if I had prayed about this decision.. She also asked me if there was anything going on in me that could be hindering my prayers. Then she said that I needed to get my own heart right with God before I judged the congregation. After all, they could be a reflection of my own lack of faith or leadership. This angered me at first. But, I knew she was right. I had forgotten the guidance from God's Word that says, 'Unless the Lord builds the house, we labor in vain.' It was apparent I was doing everything I could do as a man, and as a pastor, to build God's house, except the most important thing. God was not building this church. We were the reflection of man's work, not the reflection of God's work, and it showed by our poor spiritual health. I wanted us to look like a healthy church without being a healthy church. We had no real heart for Christ or His mission. We had lost our first love for the King, and the symptoms were apparent. The Lord had left our church, and we never knew it, for we were trying to prop it up with our programs, fund-raising efforts, and any other thing we could do to keep it alive. We were 'doing church,' but we were not 'being a church,' and there is a big, big difference."

Pastor Nate took a swallow of his tea, and continued. "The first thing I did was to get alone with God for a week. I went to a cabin in the mountains, so that I could fast and pray over the things Nelda challenged me with. I hadn't fasted and prayed like this since we surrendered to the ministry. Needless to say, I hadn't been asking the Lord how to lead, how to preach, or how to serve. I was just doing it the best I knew how, and how I had been taught. I was missing the most important ingredient needed for leadership which is the wisdom God imparts when we ask, seek, and knock on His door. I was prideful, and this had become a hindrance, and likely contagious in the congregation. Early in my week in the mountains, God revealed this problem to me, and brought me into repentance, forgiveness, and restoration. My first love for Christ was restored, as well my passion and heart for serving the people of the valley."

He went on, "The next few days in the cabin on the mountain were the best time of wonderful praise and worship of God that I have ever experienced. For the first time, I came to understand what it really means to have an intimate, abiding relationship with Jesus Christ, and it was changing my whole perspective. I was watching my life being transformed before my own eyes. I was growing in faith and expectation again, which was something that had been long lost. I was beginning to see God for Who He is, and a spirit of amazement began to take hold of me. The weight of disappointment was falling off me, and the joy of being yoked to the Lord replaced my anger and sorrow. That was the big turn-around for me, and the man who went back home to Nelda at the end of the week."

Nelda refreshed our tea, and brought out a few more teacakes for us to enjoy as Nate paused before continuing his story. I was wrapped up in it, and could see his tears as he remembered the joyful week as if it were yesterday. Obviously, something momentous occurred in him while he was on that mountain.

Pastor Nate cleared his throat, and went on. "Toward the end of the week, I began to hear God's voice. It came in the form of an assurance I never had before, and encouragement. I felt He wanted me to ask for a blessing for my church, and the valley. The people were so comfortable with their lives, it was if they didn't need God. They had Religion as their God, but they didn't really know Him as I had discovered Him on the mountain. I knew first hand there was something missing in their lives, for it had been missing in mine. Therefore, I asked of God that the people of our church, and the valley, would come to know Him as He wants to be known, and to experience the true abundance that comes from intimacy with Him. I continued to enjoy my communication with the Lord the rest of the week, and slowly I was given a powerful impression that in order for the people to be blessed, they must give up their idols. I asked, 'Lord, what idols do they have?' I was thinking of a graven image, or such."

Nate explained, "God replied, 'It is their self-sufficiency. They have forgotten Me, and they have taken My provisions for them for granted.

102

They have made their life, and their security, a god, never recognizing it is My provisions that sustain them. Their religion is a lukewarm expression of their love for Me, and I am appalled by it.' I immediately remembered the letter in The Book of Revelation," and he quoted it from memory:

> *"I know your deeds, that you are neither cold nor hot; I wish that you were cold or hot. So because you are lukewarm, and neither hot nor cold, I will spit you out of My mouth. Because you say, "I am rich, and have become wealthy, and have need of nothing," and you do not know that you are wretched and miserable and poor and blind and naked, I advise you to buy from Me gold refined by fire so that you may become rich, and white garments so that you may clothe yourself, and that the shame of your nakedness will not be revealed; and eye salve to anoint your eyes so that you may see."*

Pastor Nate kept on, "I then became frightened for the people of my church. For the first time, since I became their pastor, I began to intercede for them in earnest, and ask God to turn their hearts back to Him. I asked Him to do whatever it takes. I heard Him say to me, *'Do not be frightened by the process, for it is required to cause the people to return to Me. Because they are prideful, and convinced by their own self-righteousness, My blessings will flow to them only through the most unlikely source so they will know true worship by what they see in him. When they turn to Me with all their heart, I will heal their land, and bring them into My heart.'* I didn't understand His words, *'My blessings will flow to them only through the most unlikely source, so they will know true worship by what they see in him.'* Therefore, I asked Him what it meant. His response was, *'You will understand when you return home from these mountains.'"*

He took a breath, "That week was the beginning of a spiritual revolution in my life. But, it was also the beginning of a drought that came to the valley for the next four years, as not one drop of rain fell on the soil, except for one small area of the valley."

Nelda was ready to add her words to the story. "You need to understand the farming around here has been strictly rainfall farming. The climate around here has been so ideal because the right amount of rainfall in spring and summer always comes. It has always been this way since the fertile valley was settled. No irrigation has been needed. The fields are tilled, the seeds are planted, and the crops grow abundantly. The lush grass for hay can always be cut and bailed two or three times a year. The livestock are well fed, well watered, and provide prime milk, cheese and meat. All the food markets in the cities love to buy from this valley, for they know it is the 'best of the best.' Needless to say, the farmers in this valley had it pretty easy compared to most operations, and they didn't know what to do when their predictable climate became unpredictable and failed them."

She leaned forward, and with sadness, she explained, "The first year of the drought, they rode it out alright, and just took a break or went on vacation, and waited for the next year. Still no rain came. The second year, some of the smaller farmers had to go to the factory 60 miles away for jobs. The bigger farm owners had a little more reserves. By the third year, panic was setting in with every farmer in the valley. They were getting the message, but they didn't understand what it meant. Nate preached some red-hot sermons about repentance, but the sermons also didn't hit home. But, as the drought continued, they started to listen and the sermons began to hit the mark. Some mighty hard praying began to be heard from the church during the Wednesday night prayer meetings. The people were being shown that their 'idol of self-sufficiency' was letting them down."

When Nelda paused, I asked, "You mentioned that no rain fell in the valley for four years except one, small section. Was that Gabe's farm?"

They both nodded that it was.

Pastor Nate spoke up, "It was the most amazing thing we've ever seen, to see every farm in the valley parched and brown from the drought, but Gabe's farm green and overflowing with vegetables and fruit. It was a stark contrast, and it puzzled us all. Some people tried to explain it as Gabe's farm being in a unique position to catch a heavier than normal nighttime dew. Some tried to say because of a change in the prevailing wind, his place got rain when no other farm did. But, those theories couldn't explain a drought lasting four long years. No, there was something else going on, and it got our attention in a big way. We came to understand Gabe and his farm were being singled out by God for a blessing, while everyone and everything around him were not included in it."

"Like I said, most people in the valley didn't know Gabe. We would see him and his family at the general store, but beyond that he was an unknown. We didn't care to know them, for we had no interest. We all had the attitude that they had their ways and we had ours, and so we just don't mix. By the way," Pastor Nate emphasized, "a good way to spot cultural prejudice is when the word 'they' is used to describe somebody different from you. That was how we looked at Gabe and his family, and we thought it was likely the way they looked at us. God taught us a great lesson about how terribly displeasing this perspective is to Him, especially when it involves people of a different race in His family."

"So how did Gabe handle it? Did he get rich because he had the only farm in the valley that produced?" I laughingly asked.

"Well, there wasn't a single person in this valley who wouldn't have taken advantage of the situation if the shoe had been on the other foot. Gabe could have asked any price he wanted, and got it in the cities. He knew market pricing and the rules of supply and demand. But, that wasn't how Gabe lived his life. He was connected to Christ in a way that most of us have never experienced. I have come to learn since then, this kind of connection is available for all God's children if we will take it. Gabe had it, and he wouldn't let something like earthly treasure take from him what he had with the Treasure of the Universe. He knew he was to be a steward of the blessings God had entrusted to him, and there was a purpose for the miracle taking place on his farm, so it was not about personal prosperity."

I immediately thought, "What an indictment it is for Christians who have been blessed with great prosperity, but use it for their own selfish pleasure, rather than blessing others who are in need. Surely God must be displeased with such selfish use of His resources!"

Nate interrupted my thoughts. "Before I got to know Gabe, I visited with Burt Senior at the general store about him. Burt had all these wonderful vegetables and fruits in his bins. Now, I'm talking about prime crops one rarely sees. But, the prices were last year's prices, and were way below true market value. So I asked him where he was getting the beautiful vegetables, and how is he able to hold the prices down?"

Pastor Nate continued, "Burt Senior told me it's the strangest thing he'd ever seen. The farmer told him he would supply all the vegetables he would need, and he could take his normal markup, but there were two things he would have to agree to. He required the prices charged would have to be pre-drought prices, and if the people couldn't afford the vegetables, he would give them what they needed with no profit to either of them. Burt couldn't understand why he wouldn't at least charge the higher market price because it's just the way things are done! So he asked him why he wanted this done. The farmer told him the people in the valley were having a hard time, and they shouldn't add to their burden. Also, since the people's own gardens were not producing, they would need as many vegetables as possible for the winter so they could preserve them. He said they needed to help them the best they could by keeping prices down. Burt said he hadn't seen or heard anything like what that farmer did. He asked the farmer why he didn't take his produce to the cities, for the crops that come from this valley are like gold to the restaurants and specialty markets there. He said this was a time our own people in the valley need help in a big way."

Nate continued, "I asked Burt Senior who the farmer was, and he told me it was Gabe. I decided right then and there it was time for me to meet Mr. Gabe, so I drove immediately to his farm. When I arrived, Gabe was in the field gathering some of the harvest and putting it in the back of his mule-drawn wagon. He saw me drive up, and left the field to come to meet me."

"I really didn't know what to expect at the time," Nate said. "I had never had any friends who were black. I only knew what I had observed, which was limited, or what I had been taught, which was cultural prejudice. I was a little uneasy, for I didn't know if he would be suspicious of my being there, or angry, or frightened. But Gabe made it so easy for me. You know his smile and demeanor? You know how he greeted everyone, as if God sent that person right to him? Well, That's the way he greeted me. He welcomed me, a stranger, into his life right then and there. I'll never forget that first time I met him."

I recalled the same impression I had of Gabe. I have since found this was exactly how he felt about every stranger, or situation, that came to him. A person or problem or opportunity was God's business, and Gabe felt he should embrace it as having been permitted for a purpose that was beyond his understanding. He simply received all of us as if God had put us before him, so God could love us through him.

Nelda added her input. "When Nate came home from the mountains, I saw a new spring in his step, and I could tell he had been greatly encouraged. I knew he felt alone in his new spiritual journey, and he needed a friend to talk with, and to confide in. It's hard for a preacher in a church like ours to be transparent, and Nate had to keep his guard up. I don't think anyone would have understood at the time God was creating a renovation in his heart, and this would make him a spiritual revolutionary."

"What do you mean by the term, 'spiritual revolutionary,' Nelda?" I asked.

"Well, Nate had come away from the mountains a changed man. He had been with Christ in such a way his first love for Him had been restored, and he couldn't go back to his old ways of preaching, or to simply go through the motions as the pastor of this church. He came back with a mission and a purpose, but he didn't have a plan. He just knew a spiritual revolution had begun in his own life, and he was no longer content with religious activity. He wanted the people of our church to see Christ like we had never beheld him before. He had an excitement building within like a volcano, and it needed to be released. It helped him that day to know there was someone who lived in the valley who lived his life like Nate wanted to begin living his. In Gabe, he found that man."

"Nelda said I didn't have a plan," Pastor Nate stated. "The truth is, I was in danger of trying to take everything in my own hands and try to make something happen, which would have been just another attempt by a man to do something without God's guidance. As I got to know Gabe, he helped me understand not only the need for God's guidance, but also I needed His wisdom and strength. Gabe taught me about the tremendous effect that *Saturation Prayer* can have before we actively launch out to do God's work.

"'*Saturation Prayer*'?" I asked. "I guess I've never heard this term before. What does it mean?"

"Well, I didn't either, until Gabe introduced the concept to me," Nate admitted. "It was his way of describing it. But, actually, it has a great, theological basis, and *Saturation Prayer* became the first and most essential step we needed to take before the spiritual revolution came to the valley. Let me tell you how Gabe introduced this *Spiritual Secret* to me.

CHAPTER ELEVEN

The Secret of
Saturation Prayer

I was immersed in the story of Pastor Nate meeting Gabe for the first time. Since I had experienced the same welcome and attitude from him, I knew first hand what the pastor was saying. It was also no surprise to hear how Gabe was able to provide for a deep need the lonely pastor had, which was to find a friend and confidant who would walk with him through the difficult time he would face.

Pastor Nate led out, "I won't go into the details of getting to know Gabe the first day, but will just give you some impressions. First, every inch of his farm was planted in a wide variety of edible vegetables. It was the most abundant produce on a single piece of property I've ever seen. I asked him why he had planted so broadly, for it was obvious they were way beyond their needs and capability to harvest. Gabe just responded he felt there would be a need."

Nelda spoke up, "I saw their farm later, and realized something going on there that was more than rainfall feeding the crops. God's hands were on the crops, and it showed."

Pastor Nate added, "After Gabe and I got through the pleasantries of our introductions, I told him what Burt Senior at the general store had told me about him, and I just wanted to hear it for myself. He told me God had given him a special blessing with the farm that year for a special purpose in helping people, and he wanted to be a faithful steward of his King's farm."

"Needless to say," Nate continued, "I thought Gabe was either insane, or he had a connection with God I longed to understand and have for myself. As I got to know him, I came to understand he was logical, bright, humorous, and as sane as anyone could be. Therefore, I concluded I had found a man who represented everything I would expect to see in someone who walked closely with Christ. The package was a surprise for me. Like most people, I thought a man like this would be found in 'Who's Who of Superstars for Christ,' who fly around on holy missions in their private airplanes instead of in the form of a rural, subsistence farmer, who barely made ends meet each year."

"People like *that* ...," Nate started before stopping himself and saying with exasperation, "there I go again, putting Gabe in a category, and I'm just not talking about him being black! I'm talking about a poor farmer! Do you see how easy it is to be culturally biased? It's just part of our fallen nature! What I was trying to say is, what Gabe did were extreme acts of generosity and kindness to people who didn't know him, or who would have not done the same for him if he were in need. He did not act in the same manner as people in his economic situation would normally act. Most of us would have sold our crops to the highest bidder, or hoarded them for ourselves, especially someone who barely makes a living from year to year."

"I understand what you are trying to say, Pastor Nate," I volunteered. "The fact is, we make a lot of irrelevant distinctions about people, don't we? I think the people I have been most disappointed with are Christians who have been successful in their careers, and toward the end of their lives want to appear extremely generous. They make a big deal about their gifts and endowments, as if it were a real sacrifice on their part. If most people knew the clever ways wealthy people conserve their estates through tax breaks and endowments, they would understand there was less generosity involved and more tax savings and ego gratification. Certainly they wouldn't be as impressed with the gift percentages, for there is rarely no sacrifice or risk involved. I don't think many of *those people* ...."

I paused, "There I go with my own prejudice. I guess I better stop before I have to confess to you I have my own cultural prejudices, as well."

We both laughed, as we connected with a common understanding of how easy it is to categorize people, and judge them without mercy .... except ourselves.

"Miss Nelda," I asked, "I understand what inspired Gabe, and the way he expressed it, because I got to know him several years before he died. I know it was about his daily walk he enjoyed with Christ. But, how were you handling the changes with Pastor Nate? Were you scared about his new outlook in life and ministry?"

"I had watched a young man have a fire lit in his heart when Nate and I entered seminary, and then I watched it slowly fade to only a slight glow for the next fifteen years," Nelda answered. "There were no two people more impassioned about Christ, and the work he called us to, than Nate and me. But, there is a quagmire of religious conformity and stagnant faith within many churches that just quenches the Holy Spirit's work, and it was happening in our church in a big way. The empowering grace relationship we could have with God had been pushed aside by our religious activity. Because of this, we just died on the vine spiritually. Nate and I had lost our spiritual vitality, and we were ready to leave this valley. When he went away to pray, I did my own praying. I asked God to rekindle our hearts with His Spirit and fullness. I, too, laid it out to the Lord, and simply asked Him to send us His help. I confessed every known sin I had, and threw in a few I could have been close to, for good measure. When Nate came home, it was like seeing Moses come from the mountains with a glow on his face from being with God. He had a joy about him that spoke of hope, and trust, and passion. I knew my prayers had been answered."

"Now, concerning Gabe," Nelda continued, "from a woman's point of view, I had observed him with his wife and children before we even knew his name. He was kind with the children and affectionate with his wife. I could see there was a lot of happiness in the family, and they respected him greatly. He was a big man, and the children loved to hang on his shoulders. His family was such a joy to him, and he gave them his priority. That stood out to me like a light, for so many fathers neglect being affectionate in expressing their love to their family. Men seem to be afraid that their wife and children will lose respect for them if they show vulnerability. It didn't hurt Gabe's family, though, for they were well adjusted, and they all adored him"

Changing the subject, I asked, "Pastor Nate, would you explain to me about the *Saturation Prayer* you were talking about?"

Pastor Nate responded, "After meeting Gabe the first time, I was so impressed with him I returned to visit him often. I would take a soft drink or water to the fields while he was working, and would chat with him. Our friendship grew like his crops. Before long, I would time it so I could catch him when he had finished his field-work to not distract him from it. Since he would always joyfully leave his work to be with me, I felt I needed to respect his time. That was a back-breaking time for Gabe, for the harvest was so great. I convinced him to let me hire some out-of-work farm workers for him temporarily, and I would oversee his books to make sure it only increased the cost to the people by just a fraction. I knew this was the main reason he tried to do all the harvesting with his family. He went along with my recommendation, for he knew the produce would rot in the fields if not gathered as each crop matured."

"It was later in our friendship that I began to confide with Gabe about the state of affairs in our church, the valley and my own life.

112

I told him I saw in him someone I wanted to be like. He told me, 'You don't want to be like me; you want to be like Jesus. You can become the man you really want to be if you learn to walk closely with Him. The issue is not being like someone else. It's allowing God to make everything He wants to make of you!' He was right. It hit the heart of what I was trying to say, but he said it better."

He kept going, "I was sharing with him about my time alone with God in the mountains, and the great excitement that came out of it. I told him I felt God wanted me to do something that would dislodge the people from their spiritual rut, but I didn't have a plan. That's when he mentioned The Secret of *Saturation Prayer*. Here's how Gabe put it. He explained, 'When I was in Europe during World War II, I saw the devastating effects of the Nazi's saturation bombing on England, along with the discouragement, and challenge, for those people to rise out of the rubble. Churchill called it their "finest hour." We crossed over the Channel, and I saw the devastation of saturation bombing on the French shore-lines to prepare for the Allied troops to invade Europe. I also saw how joyful the French were for their liberation. In Germany, I saw the devastation of saturation bombing on a once arrogant and inde-pendent nation, and how it broke their will, and removed the reign of terror that was going on in their land. In each case, the people were humbled, made needy, and prepared for deliverance.'"

Nate cleared his throat and continued, "Gabe said, 'When I became a Christian and started to understand I have an invisible spiritual war constantly going on around me, I came to realize the great need for the protection and wisdom God gives to my family and me through prayer. I am convinced it is absolutely essential to our walk with Him. When I began to look outside our own needs, and to look at the condition of our extended family and friends, I applied a special kind of prayer to their needs. I called it *Saturation Prayer*. With this kind of prayer, I asked God to bombard these people with circumstances and challenges that would reveal to them their independence of Him, and to put in them a conscious and desperate need for His help, as well, the need to get to know Him better. Amazingly, I saw God bring into their lives humbling circumstances, and this made them want His help. I think of it as a

113

kind of "softening up" the enemy's position, preparing the way for a great work by God. Most of the people I prayed for were living proud and independent of God, and were ignorant of how much they had bought into Satan's lies. Ultimately, God delivered the people from their trials. But, the greatest blessing was the long-lasting effect of knowing God as they had never known Him before. The ones who made the connection with finding God through their trials, all say, it was all worth it, and they would go through them again to connect with God like they had.'"

Nate looked me in the eye and said, "Gabe then asked me, 'Nathan, have the people been living with pride in their lives, and have they been taking God's blessings for granted?' I nodded my head indicating we all had done so. 'You told me you had prayed to God, and asked Him to turn the hearts of the people of this valley toward Him, and to do whatever it takes. Do you believe this is something God would want to do for these people?'"

Nelda nodded, as Nate continued, "I sat quietly as Gabe continued his explanation. 'You said the drought started immediately after your prayer for God's intercession. Do you think this could be the beginning of your prayers being answered? Do you see how God could be removing the prideful independence from your lives, and how He is softening all of you up for a great spiritual campaign to move into this valley? Because of this, you must pray even more diligently so you do not speak from the pulpit in haste, or with a judgmental spirit. There will be a time for you to be their exhorter, by speaking with authority and conviction, and to give them leadership. But, there is still more to be done by God to prepare their hearts. God's prophet must often tear the people down to dislodge them from their hard hearts. But, he works side-by-side with God through this process. A true prophet not only teaches God's Word, he also demonstrates His heart of compassion. Therefore, you must also build the people back up after they've been torn down. Never forget this, or you will excuse ruthless behavior as inspired by God. You must understand your words of rebuke must also be accompanied by love and hope of restoration with God, or you will not be speaking with the heart of God. You must saturate this valley with prayer, and you must empty yourself of yourself, so you can be an instrument in His hands. This is what I mean by *Saturation Prayer.'"*

Back on the porch, Pastor Nate dipped his head and breathed out a silent prayer as he remembered Gabe's wisdom. I could tell his conversation with Gabe he had just shared with me was a defining moment in his life. I wanted to hear more, but the afternoon was late, and I feared overstaying my welcome.

I volunteered, "Maybe I better leave you folks, and come back later."

"Nonsense!" Nelda spoke out with authority. "You will stay and eat dinner with us. Nate has needed to pass this story along for a long time. This is good for both of us. Besides, you've only heard the build-up for the real story you are wanting to know about."

The truth is, it was only a courteous gesture on my part to the elderly couple that I offered to leave. I wanted to stay with them and hear it all. Everything they had told me gave me a good foundation for understanding the spiritual condition of the people of the valley, the "spiritual revolution" Pastor Nate was praying for, and the way God had used Gabe to reach the people.

I could feel such a powerful and encouraging message to my own heart taking place as I heard many times how God used my old mentor, without it being an outright mission. He was like a lightning rod. God's power and love flowed strongly to him and through him to other people. He astounded everybody who really knew the truth about the man.

But, he also was an enigma to us all because he was nothing special to look at, or to seek after. Instead, he was like most ordinary people you see around farms and the countryside. Even today, people like him, indifferent of race, are often overlooked. Getting to know someone like this man requires a shift in our perspective before we can get below the exterior, and to the heart of the person. I have found it helps me to consider what Jesus looked like when He lived His life out before mankind. He didn't distinguish

Himself from other people by the way He looked. If He walked in a crowd today, we wouldn't be able to identify Him as the Son of God by the way He physically appeared to us.

But, taking time to hear Him, and getting to know His heart, would declare His majesty and deity to us. Abiding with Him would literally rock our lives and our world, because what happens below the surface of our lives when our heart is connected to Him, transforms us inside out. Taking the time, and putting aside our differences, changes our perspective toward other people, and opens the door for us to get a look at hidden qualities we would have overlooked.

Gabe was a precious package wrapped in plain paper. Below the surface were great faith and a heart of gold. I believe it is people like Gabe, who have walked in the world as unsung heroes, and who live discretely away from the world's applause and stardom, who are the silent champions of their faith in God. We don't read about them, or know that they are an undercurrent of blessing to our lives, because their legacy of faith is invisible. However, occasionally God will allow some people, as happened to Nate, Nelda, and me, to observe the silent work going on behind the scenes, with such a man.

Since Dottie was away from the farm this night, I accepted Nelda's invitation, and as a result, she, Pastor Nate and I talked the rest of the afternoon, and evening. They provided me with information on the two years that followed Gabe's counsel to Nate as Gabe met regularly to *saturate* the valley with their prayers.

Before long, Nelda and Gabe's wife, Katherine, joined with them, and a family friendship began to intertwine along with their prayers. Gabe's family grew to love Nate and Nelda, and vice versa. In fact, it was Gabe's youngest daughter, Lilly, who nicknamed Nathan, "Pastor Nate." Since Pastor Nate and Nelda had no children of their own, the children came to be loved by the couple as if they were their own.

I asked Pastor Nate and Nelda if the people in the valley looked at

116

them as social activists, since it was during the 1950s, and was a heated era concerning racial tensions.

He replied, "Our friendship had nothing to do with a social statement by either family. We just loved each other, as good friends do. Sure, there were people who didn't understand how this could happen, for they hung onto their separation issues. These people might have branded us as activists. If anything, Nelda and I were Christian activists, and we tried to live faithfully by how the Word of God taught us. Social norms, or social revolutions, or political adaptation, cannot be a Christian's guide in his or her life, or we will be diverted from God's guidance. We live in a corrupt world led by imperfect people, and all of us face an evil influence every day. For that reason, we must have a trustworthy map to follow, as it will lead us in life. God's Word, and a true heart connection to Him, will break down any barrier we once had about racial separation. I saw in Gabe a man who was a spiritual brother to me, and our differences just didn't matter anymore."

Pastor Nate paused, and then continued, "Our chairman of the Elder Board and I had a little visit about my friendship with Gabe and his family. Gabe had already warned me to not get angry or hardened toward those who would challenge us about our friendship, and to be patient with them. He had lived through a lot of misunderstandings and persecution himself, and had gotten great victory over his anger. He had not allowed an unforgiving spirit to reside in his life, for he knew the poison it would become and the devastating damage is would cause. This gave him patience, and even emitted God's grace to those who were still struggling with the issues. Personally, I don't think he could have become the great man he was if he had kept a bitter, unforgiving spirit within him."

"I would agree with that," I interjected.

Nate nodded, and went on, "I asked him one day how he did it. He simply replied he didn't want to allow something evil to reside in him, and that would keep him from having an unhindered relationship with his King. He also said something else that told me he had worked through a lot personal struggles, and therefore, he understood how anger and bitterness could be reproduced in his family. He said he wanted his children to never carry any bitterness that remained in him into their lives, and it needed to stop with him."

I wondered what Gabe meant by that.

Nate explained, "Gabe told me, 'I fear there will come a day that angry black leaders will lead many in my race astray, by making them agitated because of their bitterness toward white people. They will do this so they can keep control of their followers, and manipulate them for their own selfish purposes. By keeping this anger and unforgiveness alive, an angry person will follow an angry leader. These people will never find the true freedom they want if they keep bitterness in them. Katherine and I want our children to understand this and be prepared for it, by the way we live our life out before them. Social reform is needed, and should come. But it will not bridge the division between the black and white people in this nation. There must be a spiritual awakening in both races that offers both repentance and forgiveness, to find reconciliation. Most of all, in the body of Christ, we must stop looking at our differences, and focus on what we have in common in Christ. We must fix our eyes on Christ Who transforms our hearts, and allow His peace to reign in us. Then, harmony will come between the races, and the benefit we all want will follow.' There was incredible wisdom in his words."

Pastor Nate reflected on what Gabe had spoken over thirty years before, and stated in a sober voice, "Gabe was a prophet, and it looks like his fears have been realized."

We all remained quiet, as we reflected on the obvious racial tensions in our nation. These tensions have birthed angry leaders of both races, who, although opposed to one another, are very similar in their own propaganda of hate and hypocrisy against the other. I felt that Gabe had hope there would be godly leaders of both races who will be raised up, and will lead God's family to the true freedom that comes from granting forgiveness and giving justice, mercy and grace.

I brought our attention back to the chairman of the elders who Pastor Nate had mentioned by asking, "What did the elder say to you?"

Pastor Nate responded, "Well, first let me say he was a good man, and wanted to keep peace within the church. This was his first concern. But, he was also a man familiar with the hypocrisy that existed there, and a conflict of belief in pre-judging another man because of the color of his skin. God was dealing with him on this important issue. I'm not surprised, because part of God's work in response to our *Saturation Prayer* was to prepare the hearts of His people, and it was obvious to me this was taking place. Like Gabe suggested, I didn't react to his questions, but simply began to share with him about my prayer in the mountains for the people of the valley, and how I was eventually brought to Gabe. Since it was a secret in the valley about the produce being provided by him and he hadn't heard about Gabe or his deal with Burt Senior, I brought him up-to-date on everything. After he heard my story, he asked to meet with Gabe to hear his perspective. I arranged a time for the three of us to meet, and then just let him and Gabe talk. Before long, he had the same feelings I did about Gabe, the problems going on in the valley, and what needed to happen. He joined us in our *Saturation Prayer* efforts, and never missed a meeting. He brought his wife along, and then there were six of us praying in earnest."

By this time, we were finished with dinner, and had moved to the front porch again to enjoy Nelda's delicious dessert. I knew there was more to the story, and it was about to culminate in a dramatic finish. Before entering the final phase of Pastor Nate's and Nelda's story, I came to understand their church at the time was still stand-offish from coming to grips with their cultural prejudice toward Gabe and his family, even though some of the people had found out that Gabe and his farm were the benefactors of the life-preserving crops they were receiving. God was working on them inside out, and it was simply a matter of time until this issue would be addressed. The drought had lingered into its fourth year. Individuals and families were being affected personally and financially, as well being led to much-neglected truth.

There is a common *people dynamic* that consistently occurs when people suffer together in a mutual problem. As they grow closer to each other for comfort, walls of separation fall. Pastor Nate's church had begun a radical transformation of its heart and spirit, as the people joined together pleading with God for answers and His help. Brokenness and fear drove the people to repentance, and this resulted in greater harmony among them. Songs and liturgy were no longer sung and quoted by meaningless repetition. The words came alive to the people, and spoke words of comfort and conviction to the congregation. The church was now being church, rather than doing church, and the families praying for this reformation were assured that God was at work answering their prayers.

Pastor Nate was then able to preach powerful messages of repentance and oneness with Christ. The church members were now ready, as Gabe had promised, to welcome his words. His preaching stung their hearts, and his messages produced fruit of conviction and repentance. Life change was unfolding.

But, the drought lingered on, for there was still an insidious perspective God wanted to root out of His people. The continued drought kept them seeking for answers, until it became clear that an abandonment of their cultural norms, and a change in their attitude were required. No longer was God content with their token admissions and distant involvement. It was now at a point that a drastic change in direction, one way or the other, would be required. Remaining *status quo* would no longer be a comfortable option to choose. A challenge was given requiring them to make a stand and risk all, or walk in complete defiance and disobedience to God. However, sitting on the fence would become a very uncomfortable position for any member, if Reverend Nathan Schumacher remained the church's pastor.

I was on the edge of my seat as Nelda and Pastor Nate shared the remaining events that took place in their story. In its climactic end, I was able to hear how deliverance from an evil tyranny was overcome, followed by healing and restoration in the valley. As I listened, I could not help but apply the truths of the story to my own life, its relationships, my church, and my nation.

CHAPTER TWELVE

The Secret that
Abandonment &
Trust Forge Courage

O n their front porch, Nelda continued the story by saying, "Now, you need to understand what was happening, and the attention it brought to Gabe's farm. This whole valley had turned to dust, except his 80 acres that was producing crops on a supernatural level. He wasn't selling them to the merchants in the cities, which made them mad and suspicious. This is when greedy people start to scheme, which was the case with a rich landowner in the next county. He had been trying to snatch up land in the valley for some time, but somehow people stayed together and wouldn't break even though times were tough. He really wanted to buy Gabe's farm, and offered him top dollar, but Gabe wasn't interested. He then started his scheming as to how he could get Gabe off the farm so he could get it. He reasoned Gabe was isolated from the rest of the people in the valley, and it wouldn't take much to scare him off. That's when he started rumors about Gabe."

"Rumors?" I asked. I hadn't expected that.

"Yes, we got word one Saturday he was stirring up some men over in the next county by telling lies about Gabe, and something was supposed to happen the following night. The word was out, and the rich man's head-bangers were sending a message that this was none of our business, and no one would get hurt if we would just turn off our lights, go to bed, and stay out of it. If we didn't listen to their threat, they would come after us. All of us in the valley got the message, and were scared to death. The next Sunday, Nathan put his prepared message aside, and instead spoke from his heart. It was the most powerful message I have ever heard, and it put everyone on notice this would be a defining time in their lives by how they reacted to it."

Nelda paused, looked at Nate, and asked, "Do you want to take it from here?"

"Well, the message included my resignation," Pastor Nate responded. "I made it clear to the congregation this was a time that complacency was not an option. I had already gotten rumblings all of them had decided to stay out of it, and based on the expressions I saw on their faces, they hadn't changed their minds. I had been praying hard, asking the Lord to give me the insight I needed and words the congregation should hear, before I spoke to them. God told me to let His Word speak to them, and then gave me three key passages to use."

"What were the they?" I asked.

Nate answered, "The first one was Psalms 1:1-3."

I knew the verses by heart:

"Blessed is the man who does not walk in the counsel of the wicked or stand in the way of sinners or sit in the seat of mockers. But his delight is

in the law of the Lord, and on his law he meditates day and night. He is like a tree planted by streams of water, which yields its fruit in season and whose leaf does not wither. Whatever he does prospers."

Nate continued, "After I read it, I then went on to ask the congregation several questions which left them wide-eyed and shocked. 'Have you ever wondered why Gabe's farm has never failed to produce while all of ours has been dust fields for four years? Could God be trying to give us all a message that Gabe might have a special connection with Christ none of us has? Could there be something God is saying to us that we must do in order to break the back of the drought on our land, and why we might be having it in the first place? Is one man living his life in such a way that Jesus delights in him, and prospers him in spite of the drought? What can we learn from this? And the two biggest questions are, have we been living our lives in such a way that leaves God out? And, have we gotten so smug in our success, our comfortable lives, our pride, and even our religiosity in this church that God left us long ago, and we didn't even miss Him being gone?'"

"You should have seen their faces," Nelda added.

Nate chuckled, "I got some sober stares because of that last question. I didn't know if they were listening more intently or if they were trying to figure the best way to push me out of the doors, so I decided they needed to know some things Gabe had done that caused God to delight in him. I started by letting them in on the secret of how they had been able to buy vegetables for their freezers at a price that no one could understand. I told them about his generosity and concern for them. I told them how godly he and his wife were, and how they lived their lives faithfully before the Lord. I challenged them on the cultural and racial bias they had against this black family who lived in their valley. I told them of the years they had prayed for everyone in this valley, even though not one of them was willing to even introduce himself or herself to them, much less pray for them. I asked the church if God could be giving them a message, for I knew He was giving me one. Their silence was deafening as they hung their heads in shame."

123

"You know what I think?" Nate asked as he looked at me. "I think up until this time, our people had no concept God communicates to us in such a way. They were believers who thought God was really not involved with the fortunes, or the failures, of His people. They just accepted the fact they were lucky to live in a fertile valley that reproduced bountiful crops every season. They could understand how a climate change affects a region because it happens all the time in other parts of the world, and how it could even happen to their valley. But, the situation they had been experiencing the last four years was very mysterious, for Gabe's crops never failed while everyone else's crops in the valley around him had failed. I knew ahead of time they would be shocked, and even angered, when I made a spiritual connection to this mystery. That's why I had my resignation ready."

I laughed at this admission by Pastor Nate, although I realized it was a serious time for him to put his job in jeopardy in order to speak truth to his congregation. It was not an aimless gesture. He had placed before the people a point of decision, which required a choice.

He went on to say to me, "Gabe said when a prophet speaks to his people, he might very well be required to speak in such a way it tears down and breaks hardened hearts. I came to see I had to speak truth, and let it sting. I could see in their faces they were full of shame. But, Gabe also said a prophet must build the people back up, after he tears down. So I gave them the second passage in order to give them hope. I read 2 Chronicles 7:14."

We quoted it together:

"If my people, who are called by my name, will humble themselves and pray and seek my face and turn from their wicked ways, then will I hear from heaven and will forgive their sin and will heal their land."

Nate kept going without a pause, "When I read that verse, I could see their heads lift, as if a surge of hope had been breathed into them, and a promise of healing had been given. A little hope goes a long way, provided we do our parts. Therefore, I quoted my last verse from Joshua 24:15 in order to help them understand action was needed to be taken on their part."

I didn't know the verse by heart, but it was a good one:

"But if serving the Lord seems undesirable to you, then choose for your-selves this day whom you will serve, whether the gods your forefathers served beyond the River, or the gods of the Amorites, in whose land you are living. But as for me and my household, we will serve the Lord."

Pastor Nate continued sharing the words he spoke to his congrega-tion that Sunday. "There comes a time and place when a decision is required to follow God's way or the way of evil. Rarely do we see lines drawn so clearly, as we do now. Yes, we have a threat against us. But, there is always a threat when we follow the Lord's way. There is risk, and there is no guarantee God will deliver us from the very thing we fear. But, if there is no risk, faith is not required. Our plans may fail. But God has a better plan for us, and surely when we ask our Father for a fish, He will not give us a serpent! God has assured us He will stand beside His faithful children who depend on Him. God will help us overcome our enemy in His own way. He *will* give strength to the weak and courage to the fearful, if we will only rely on Him. I repeat: He *will* do these things! We can trust Him to do so, for He is *always* faithful and trustworthy. But, in order for Him to come and do these things in our lives, we *must* take risks, and we *must* declare to the world by the way we live our lives that we will serve the Lord no matter what happens to us! In all cases, God's men and women must stand firm against evil! Remember: *our King stands with us, and He will prevail!*"

Nate paused, as he likely did when he first gave this all-important message to his congregation. Part of me wished I had been in the church that day, and part of me was glad I wasn't.

Then Nate continued, as if he were still preaching that sermon, "As many, if not all, of you know, we have received word there will be a ruthless gang of thugs who will be showing up at Gabe's farm tonight with the intention of running him and his family out of the valley. We were told we should stay out of it. We were told to not involve ourselves in it, or they will come after us. We were told to go inside our homes, hide our eyes, and act like nothing was happening, so we would not see their evil, or stand against it. We were told this family is not one of our own, and they don't belong here. How does that strike you? Can you think of any man and his family who deserve to belong here more than Gabe and his? Is there any one of us who has lived his life in such a way that we demonstrate our love for our neighbors by the way we serve them, better than Gabe and his family? I haven't."

I was seeing Gabe in a whole new light, and yet it sounded so much like him.

Nate was still talking, "If you are honest with yourselves, you haven't either. But, I can say without hesitation, this family has! So, here are my questions to you: Will you follow the voice of evil that tells you to 'stay home,' or will you follow the voice of God that says, 'stand firm'? Will you take a stand against this tyranny and the evil that seeks to devour the life of a godly, innocent man, or will you close your eyes, and think in doing so you can stay safe and far away from it? Will you stand with Christ as He stands with Gabe, or will you hide in fear, and hope this evil doesn't come near you? Will you hang your heads in shame and defeat, and not venture out to the valley where a giant awaits you as the young shepherd boy, David, did, or will you stay out of harm's way, and only watch from afar the courage of another man? Will you deny yourselves the opportunity to see your God defend you, and fight for you, or will you miss it? Will you battle for this man Gabe and his family, and ultimately find a courageous heart beating within you, or will you comfort yourself by believing this family is not one of us? Will you harden your heart and live in your fear, or will find your heart and follow your King to face a giant — an evil giant — who comes to this valley tonight?"

Pastor Nate continued to recite his sermon of several years past like it was only yesterday. He finished it up be saying, "I tell you the truth, if you think this evil will not come after you, you are mistaken. Evil has been in this valley for a long time, and has prepared the way for the gang of thugs who will show up tonight.

Evil has been unseen, and working against you like a hidden cancer that is also unseen, until it is too late. But, evil is showing itself now. Tonight is its coming out party! But, this is also a night that evil can be dispatched, and healing brought to our land, if we will join together and stand firm against it. We must stand together for righteousness, and stand against this evil! We cannot run from it! You will not be able to run to your homes and hide your eyes, for as surely as I stand before you now, this evil will be knocking on your door next. It will find its way into your life, and will rot you from the inside out, just like your land has rotted. It has clear intentions. It wants to destroy all of us, one at a time, beginning with Gabe, for he is the man who has been standing in the gap for us until we begin living out the faith we declare we have. We must not only fight this evil against Gabe and his family, but most assuredly for ourselves, as well. We can stand against it, and with God's help we will prevail against it. But God forbid any of us has to stand alone, like some of you are willing for Gabe to do."

Too bad the original sermon hadn't been recorded to CD! I would have listened to it, cut it apart, and studied it for hours.

Pastor Nate was still preaching, "Will God be outdone if we don't show up? Not in the slightest! If no one shows up tonight, God will still be there, as well as an invisible, powerful force, and He will surround Gabe, his family, and his land. Yes, Gabe needs us to be with him and his family tonight, but much more, we need to be with them, and find this Jesus he knows better than we do. We need the blessing that can come to us by standing for righteousness, especially in the face of this evil. So I ask you, will you stand with us tonight? Will you stand with us tonight, and watch our God prevail? The decision is yours. Nelda and I have made our choice. We will stand firm against the evil that stalks by night. We do not know the outcome of this, nor what God will allow. We only know our God is good, faithful and trustworthy, and we are going to trust His plan, whatever it is. What you decide is between you and the Lord. But, as for me and my house, we will serve the Lord!"

When Pastor Nate finished sharing with me the challenge he had made to the their congregation, Nelda spoke up. "They were stunned, and remained silent. Nate gave the most powerful message I have ever heard. But, they only hung their heads in shame. To his credit, Nate extended to them grace, and didn't shame them, or try to persuade them against their will. He simply stood, gave his resignation to the Chairman of the Elder Board, and he walked out of the building. I left with Nate, so the Chairman had to take over the service. Later, we heard the meeting went on for a long time that afternoon. As far as Nate and I were concerned, we felt they had made their choice to stay out of it, and we had made ours to stand with Gabe and his family. We were disappointed that the elder who had been praying with us didn't say anything, when Nate made his plea. But, we also knew he would have a lot to lose by declaring his convictions to the congregation. On our part, we had no condemnation toward anyone in the congregation or the elder and his wife. We just had a sorrowful feeling they were still living in a wilderness of fear and desperation. Nate and I had been released from it, and we were willing to follow God wherever He led us, even to Gabe's farm to face the evil that would arrive later that night."

I sat in a state of silent shock as the story unfolded before me, because I was thoroughly into it. In my mind's eye, I could see the faces of the congregation, and was even frightened thinking of the challenge Pastor Nate had lain out before them. It would have been was a heavy, heavy time in the history of this church and the valley.

To look at the little man and woman who shared the story, I would have never guessed that such courage could emerge from the two of them. But, I also knew courage like I was hearing about, comes from a supernatural source that is indefinable by the World's view, nor is it limited to the strong of mind and body. No! It was apparent God had supplied the courage to the pastor and his wife who made their stand that day.

Nelda and Pastor Nate told me they went home after church and packed an overnight bag, and later in the afternoon, they went to Gabe's house. She also cooked food and cookies for themselves, Gabe and his family, for her gift of hospitality was never out of use, even in such a dire situation. I asked them where the Law was in all of this, and was told the wealthy man had bribed a corrupt county sheriff to look the other way. So there was no help from local law enforcement.

I also asked if Gabe had been told about the visit that would come later that night. Pastor Nate said he had spoken to him as soon as he had heard about it the day before, and as expected, Gabe said he would not leave his farm.

"I saw no anger or fear in the man," Nate explained. "His only comment was, 'Well, it's a change to be able to look evil in the eye, rather than having it sneaking up on me from the rear. That tells me this threat is more about our overcoming the fear to run, rather than staying put. I think staying put, and trusting the Lord, is my battle plan. You'd be surprised how false courage dwindles when you just look it in the eye, and face it down.'"

Pastor Nate admitted that at the time when Gabe said this to him, he didn't really know how important his battle plan would be until later that night. When he saw it in action, it would stand out in his mind for the rest of his life.

He then shared, "Nelda and I left our house and spent the afternoon with Gabe and Katherine. Their children played outside, unaware of the threat that would be coming that night. I couldn't detect a change in Gabe's demeanor, although Katherine had an uncharacteristic quietness about her. My stomach was churning and I was dreading sundown, for I knew evil would be on its way. I did everything I could to convince Gabe to leave and, instead allow me go to the federal authorities. I assured him he wasn't a coward, or shouldn't be ashamed. He just looked at me in a sort of understanding, sympathetic way. Strange he could be in such a place as he was with the threats, and the only thing I could detect was he felt sorry for me. I asked him, 'Gabe, don't you understand these are evil, evil men who are coming here tonight, and they could kill you? At bare minimum, they will hurt you badly!'"

I wanted to know what Gabe had said in return.

Nate said, "But Gabe just continued his sympathetic stare at me as I pleaded with him to leave. 'What good does it do to stay?' I asked him. 'What does it accomplish? It can't just be about the farm, can it?'"

"Finally," Nate went on, "Gabe moved from his stare, and spoke with a gentle kindness that made me understand he wasn't just answering the question. Instead, he was opening my heart to something I didn't understand. 'No, it's not just about the farm. God has given this farm to me, and He can take it away at any time and by any means He chooses. It's about something far more important to me, which is to trust Him. I told you I have only one battle plan, which is to trust Him. If I run, what does this say about my trust in Him? If I'm not here when He shows up, what does this say about my trust in His battle plan? Nate, God will do His part. But, He has always required me to do my part, which is to trust Him. Do you understand this?'"

I was sitting forward in my chair, not wanting to miss any detail.

Nate continued, "I told Gabe that I understood, and with a break in my voice, I added, 'I am staying with you through this. But, this could be our doom, if God doesn't come through. There is no other person in this valley who will stand with us. We are by ourselves. I am frightened, and I admit it. I am not a courageous man like you. I've never been in a fight. I've always run from one. I've never depended on God like you are talking about. I say I trust Him, but I've always had a back door escape plan in case He didn't come through. But you don't even have a back door for us to run out of! This is the hardest thing I've ever been asked to do.'"

"Gabe reached out, touched my shoulder, and said with a smile, 'Pastor Nate, my dear friend. You are one of the most courageous men I have ever known. You have been willing to face your own demons and prejudices. You have laid your career, reputation and your livelihood on the line by letting everyone know where you stand in this situation. You have challenged everyone in this valley to look inward and see the great separation keeping them from God's blessings. You need not do anything else to prove your courage to God or to me. This is my battle, and you do not have to stay here any longer. You have done enough already.'"

I smiled.

Nate did too. He continued, "I knew Gabe was giving me a gracious permission to leave. I answered him directly, 'You don't understand, Gabe. I'm not staying because you asked me to be here with you. I'm staying because God has.' With that, Gabe smiled at me, and said, 'Well then, why don't you and I start talking about what happens when God reveals Himself, instead of what we will do if He doesn't? You know, we've been doing some mighty big praying for a long time now. Do you think God might be bringing things to a head? Maybe we need to trust Him with the fact this little shindig might be bigger than all of us. Maybe the stage is being set for the King to receive His glory, and some people to find the freedom we've been asking for them.'"

Pastor Nate confessed to me, "Man, did that infuse courage in me when Gabe helped me look at the positive possibilities, rather than thinking there would be nothing but bad things happening that night. I was so bound for doom because of my pragmatic, fearful thinking, I couldn't see any outcome, but a bad one. Then, in a moment, my perspective began to change, as I started to look at this situation with a new lens, the lens of faith. You see, that's what happens when a man lives a life of *Abandonment and trust in Christ. It forges courage in him,* and it infuses courage in others. Gabe just couldn't see any way possible that God's will wouldn't be carried out."

This reminded me of Shadrach, Meshach and Abednego when they told King Nebuchadnezzar that, even if they burned up in the superheated furnace, they would not bow to him.

Nate was saying, "Gabe showed me he believed with all his heart the outcome of the night would not be the decision of evil men. Instead, God would intervene in a way He would choose, and Gabe was willing to bet his life on it. Never had I felt better about how I would die, and who I would die with, if God chose to allow it, than I was feeling right then!"

As I listened to their amazing story, I could not help but empathize with the human drama of what these two families were going through at the time. I had also known a family who had faced a similar situation when thugs had repeatedly shot into their home one night, forcing the man, his wife and family to lie on the floor to keep from being killed. It was not a racial thing, for the man was white, and the shooters white, as well. But, the seedy characters involved did their evil work toward this man and his family, as they had done with black families for many years. They did not buckle, for an amazing reaction occurred, as God drew friends and citizens who opposed the action to surround the fearful family. They comforted them by standing with them and against the evil done. When this happened, the silent spectators standing in the middle were forced to choose a side, and in doing so the evil gang was overthrown, and their cause defeated. What was happening to Gabe and his family was similar in some ways, but different in others, for no one else stood with these two families. They were completely alone, except for each other, and God.

Nelda took the story from Nate, and continued, "Katherine and I were pretty quiet, as we listened to Nate and Gabe. I, too, was frightened. I tried to get Katherine to open up about her fears, but, rather than being fearful, she was as solid as a rock with her faith in Jesus, and in Gabe's leadership. She knew he would have to make a stand. She told me she would rather have his life be taken than his faith. I misunderstood what I was seeing. She wasn't fearful, more like ... prayerful. She was a powerful woman of prayer, and that was how she was processing it."

She went on, "We were listening to the men that afternoon when Nate asked Gabe what happened that would cause a man to do such evil against his neighbor. He also wanted to know what to expect since he had never been to war like Gabe had, nor had ever been mistreated because of his color or race."

"What did Gabe say?" I asked.

Nelda answered, "I'll never forget it. Gabe looked both of us in the eye, and said, 'The men who are coming tonight are terrorists. Don't be fooled into thinking otherwise. Whether they wear a white hood, a swastika, or a bandana over their face, they are still terrorists.' Then Gabe added, 'Now, you need to know this about a terrorist. A terrorist is, at his heart, a coward. He hides behind a cause, and joins a group because he is afraid to go against the crowd or to have an individualistic opinion. He needs a cause to feel better about himself and to be accepted, because deep down he knows he is a coward. He doesn't want to be seen as one, and he needs something, or someone, to prop himself up.'"

Nelda paused only briefly, and then stated, "Gabe went on to say, 'Terrorists are basically naive. Some of them are flat out ignorant, others have been misled by the leader. They don't know all that is going on, and are under someone else's control. The one who organizes a terrorist clan, or group, or whatever you want to call it, likely has a personal agenda that his followers don't know about. It's not their cause he's interested in. It's his own. He makes people mad and stirs them up, so he can keep them mad, and under his control. He then turns that anger and ignorance toward a foe, so he can achieve what he's really after. Some terrorists are also victims, even those coming tonight. They can be turned, if truth can break through to them.'"

Nate spoke up, "I noticed that Gabe lowered his voice so the children couldn't hear him, and he said, 'Know this, there is something behind the scenes going on here tonight, and it's not about us being black or causing trouble for the people around here. It's being sold this way by their leader. But, there is something else not being told to the rest of the gang. One thing for sure, what is stirring these people up is not a man, but an evil power that inspires the leader.'"

Nelda said, "I asked Gabe if this were true, what must be done to face these deceived people, and to get the truth out about what is really taking place. He told me we have to let God bring His light to the Darkness, and it will illuminate the blind followers. When I asked him what he meant, he told me the men coming that night would come in Darkness, but God would shine His Light on them, and when this happens, Darkness will show itself for what it really is. Then he quoted a passage from Isaiah that says: *'And I will bring the blind by a way that they knew not; I will lead them in paths that they have not known: I will make darkness light before them, and crooked things straight. These things will I do unto them, and not forsake them.'* After quoting the passage, Gabe remained quiet."

"Did you both understand the symbolism Gabe was using in his answer?" I asked of both Nelda and Pastor Nate.

"I knew the passage, for I had preached on it a few times," Pastor Nate volunteered. "But, it's really easy to talk about it from an historical, Biblical point of view. It's very easy to talk the theory of faith and trust, and preach on it. But, it's a whole different issue, to put your life in God's care and rely on His Word and promises with such *abandon and trust*. I was watching a man *courageously* putting all he had on the line, believing God would come through for him. I had never seen such faith. Yes, we understood the symbolism, and the implication, for we were being asked by God to join it."

"How did this make you feel?" I asked.

"Well, at first it scared me," Nate replied. "But, little-by-little I began to see that a man of faith is formed in such a time as this. God is at work in this kind of person to help others who have been mere spectators in the Christian life to become *courageous* warriors for Christ, as well. These people live by *courage and in reckless abandon* because they believe Christ walks right beside them. They trust their sovereign King to keep His word, and to allow only what He permits to come into their life. They live life with the greatest of liberation, for they would rather die in the arms of Christ knowing a smile is on His face, than live in fear and denial of Him, or be ashamed of their own fear. Did I want it? You bet I did! But, I had to take God on His terms, if I was to become this kind of man. Thank the Lord, I had a breakthrough."

"What do you mean, 'a breakthrough'?" I said, trying to make sure I understood each detail.

"There comes a time the fear of death is overcome by the victory of *abandonment*," Nate responded. "When we *abandon* our rights to ourselves, and agree with God to trust Him absolutely, there will come a breakthrough in *courage*. It's nothing like I had ever known before. It was not a bravado that sought attention for itself. It was more like what I think Jesus wanted Peter to understand when he briefly walked on the water before sinking. It is a courage that transcends our fear, and looks beyond those risks, into the pleased, smiling eyes of Christ. I knew my King was delighted. This made me *courageous*, as I could never have understood it before. That is what I mean when I say I had 'a breakthrough'."

I couldn't wait any longer to hear the climax to the story Nelda and Nate had been sharing with me all afternoon and evening. I appreciated their build-up to it, for I needed to get a good picture of the things that had occurred, not only with the two couples and Gabe's family, but also their congregation and the people of the valley. Therefore, I asked Nelda and Nate, "Please tell me about what happened that night."

CHAPTER THIRTEEN

The Secret of
Divine Illumination

Nelda and Pastor Nate could sense my desire to get to the confrontation that happened the night they had been describing. They quickly shared the afternoon had been spent in anticipation of the night. Along with prayer, the children were all bathed, fed and put in bed as the evening approached. They were also told there would be a group of men showing up after dark], and to stay in bed. The couples tried to eat a little food at sunset. Only Gabe was able to eat.

The couple told me they were all on the front porch drinking coffee about 10:00 p.m. when the first trucks turned into the gravel drive leading to the house. Slowly, several trucks and cars followed each other down the drive, and gathered a short ways from the barn and house. Nate said they could hear the vehicle doors open and close, and they could see torches being lit. He estimated about 20 men were in the pack.

I asked, "What did you do then?"

Nate responded, "Gabe stood up from his chair, hugged Katherine, and walked toward the gathering crowd. I hugged Nelda and followed Gabe. I caught up with him and asked him what he planned to do. He said he would give the Lord an opportunity to shine His light on the situation. He then winked at me, and said, 'Now, Nate, stay cool. There are some mighty impressionable people in that pack, and you don't want to lose your witness.'"

I laughed at the irony of Gabe's humor in a situation like they were in.

Nate continued, "Gabe went on to tell me, 'Our visitors needed to see in us a confidence in Christ, and we shouldn't fight anger with anger, or threats with threats. We listen, respond, and let Christ reveal His light.'"

Pastor Nate then explained what happened next, as Gabe approached the men. "'Well, men, we heard you were coming. What can I do for you?' Gabe asked them directly."

Pastor Nate commented, "Gabe had already told me a group like this would have a spokesman, but he wouldn't be leading the herd. The true leader would stay behind the scenes and whisper instructions to his spokesman. Sure enough, the man who spoke up looked at a man next to him before answering. 'Get out of this valley, is what you can do!' the spokesman shouted. 'If you pack your belongings and family and get out of the valley right now, you won't get hurt. Otherwise, all of you will get hurt, including you,' and he pointed to me."

"I wasn't feeling so cool, I'll admit," Nate explained, "but Gabe coolly replied to the gang, 'Now, what have I ever done to any of you men that would make you come here tonight and make such a demand?'"

That's a fair questions to ask.

Nate continued, "The spokesman consulted his silent leader, and then replied, 'You've been practicing some kind of witchcraft and voodoo religion. You have this valley all dried up, except for your farm. You and your black magic have got to go, or we'll burn you out!' Gabe looked at me with an I-told-you-so look, and said to the gang, 'So that's it? Somebody has gotten all you men riled up in thinking black magic has made my farm productive and the rest of the valley dry? Is that what I'm hearing'"

"It was just like Gabe had said," Nate explained. "I don't think most of those men knew why they were there. They were told some black farmer was going to be run out of the valley because he was practicing black magic. They didn't know the truth, or the motivation for the rumor that had been started about Gabe. I could see Gabe skillfully drawing out the truth. He was cool, and he was unafraid. It was if he knew what would unfold before it happened. I could see he wanted to isolate the 'joiners' from the instigators. Identifying the reason they were there, and the lie they followed, were his first steps. Gabe went on to say, 'Men, I put my hope and trust in Jesus Christ, and Him alone. He has blessed this farm for some reason, but it's not black magic. Black magic is not welcome here. Besides, I think you're putting too much trust in what the devil can do. What makes you think he would grow crops better than Jesus?' punctuating his question with a laugh. 'Who would tell you such lies?'"

Nate commented further, "I could see some division developing in the crowd with this new information, and Gabe's last question identified the person behind the hidden purpose. The instigator no doubt expected Gabe to run from the threatening crowd instead of facing them. They didn't count on him standing firm with confidence, and giving a counter claim. I thought it was a good time for me to speak up. So, I told them I was the pastor of the Lutheran Church in the valley, and I had known Gabe and his family as friends and prayer partners for a good while. I said I knew it to be true that Gabe and his family were deeply committed Christians. I also told them Gabe had been generous with the people of the valley with his produce, and that they need have no fear that evil was practiced on this farm. Instead, the only evil present is what is behind the lie they had been told. I could tell these words put a wedge in the group, as some of the torches began to be lowered, and men began to back away from others in the group."

Nate paused, then said, "I asked Nate if they had hoods or masks on and if he could identify any of them, but he told me they wore no masks, but it was dark and they were in the shadows, so they couldn't be seen clearly. Even so, he could tell there were no local valley men in the group. He really didn't know anyone he could see, and the true leader of the bunch stayed out of sight, and hid in the darkness. When I told the men these things about Gabe, someone in the back of the group spoke up and asked, 'Josh, did you know this?' I took it that Josh was the spokesman, because he answered, 'You can't trust what he's saying to you. Sure, he'll deny it. But how else can you explain his farm and the rest of the valley. You know what Vernon told us, and he knows a man that knows all about this first hand.'"

Nate touched my hand, and said with a faint smile, "Gabe looked at me and winked again, then whispered to me, 'A little light is starting to shine on the situation, and the motive behind the lie is showing up. Nate we are seeing a *Divine Illumination*. Watch where the Lord takes it.' Someone in the back of the crowd called out, 'Vernon, is that right?' The man in the shadows shook his head, knowing his obscurity had been uncovered. He had been directing the mob behind the scenes, and letting others do his dirty work, so he could deny it if he had to."

Pastor Nate sat up straight. "Before Vernon could say anything, Gabe called out, 'Vernon Stockton, is that you?' Now, the whole crowd became uneasy when they heard Gabe call Vernon by name. Then they really came unglued by the next thing Gabe said. 'Mr. Stockton, the last time I saw you a few weeks ago, you wanted to buy my place — You even offered me top-dollar for it, but I turned you down. The year before that, you tried to buy my place and I turned you down that time, as well. I guess you're not trying to buy it anymore. Are you telling these men some lies about me in order to get this place another way?'"

140

"The mob became divided," Nate recalled, "and someone in the crowd hollered out, 'Stockton, what are you up to? I didn't know you had been trying to buy this place. I've seen you work behind the scenes before to get your way, and I know how you are, and how you lie and cheat. I don't want anything to do with what you're doing here!'"

Nate added, "That man then came to the front of the crowd, threw his torch on the ground, and said to Gabe, 'Mr. Brown, I'm sorry I got mixed up in this. I've heard about how you've helped these people around here, and that you're a good man. That Vernon Stockton is a liar and a cheat. We all know it.' After he spoke to Gabe, he turned and walked to his truck to leave. Several men walked toward us, and threw their torches on the ones on the ground, too, while nodding to Gabe their agreement. They also headed toward their vehicles. About half the men from the mob drove away. But, there were still about ten really bad ones left."

I was in the scene, as it played out in my mind. Pastor Nate and Nelda had done a wonderful job of preparing me for the showdown they telling me about. I sensed a great victory had been won so far, but the worst part was still ahead.

Pastor Nate continued his account, "Vernon Stockton was a ruthless businessman, and was accustomed to getting his way. He was flushed out into the light now, so he decided to strong-arm Gabe with more severe threats and racial remarks. Gabe didn't let it faze him. He just stood firm, and brave. Stockton began to urge the men who stayed with him by telling them he would make it worth it to them to run Gabe off his farm and out of the valley. He was turning the men again, and it was starting to look very perilous for Gabe and me. This Stockton was a dangerous man who was under an influence of great evil. He was able to manipulate men into his schemes by appealing to their prejudices, just like Gabe said would happen. While this was going on, Gabe looked at me, and said, 'Nate, you ought to leave now. It's about to get real bad, unless the Lord does something fast.'"

"I mustered a short, 'I am with you until the end,' and then asked what I needed to do. Gabe asked me, 'What do you believe God would have you do, Brother Nate?'"

Nate volunteered, "I'll be honest with you. I didn't know what to do. I had been prepared for the ministry my entire adult life. I didn't know how to fight. I ran from fights. I didn't know what to say to angry men I was looking at. Somehow, I knew anything I would say would be ridiculed or sneered at by them. But, when they started walking toward us with torches and clubs in hands, the first thing that came to my Lutheran pastor's brain was a hymn we had sung in the valley for years. I just squeaked out the first few lines of it as loud as I could: *'A mighty fortress is our God, a bulwark never failing ...'"*

Nate went on, "It shocked the men in their steps at first, and they stopped in their tracks. Then, they started laughing at me before I could go any further with the song."

I could imagine how the mob ridiculed Pastor Nate's battle song.

"They mocked my faith and cursed me for being with Gabe, but then Gabe looked at me with a great smile and said, 'Nate, let's finish that verse together.' So, we sang the rest of the verse loudly together. *'our helper He, amid the flood of mortal ills prevailing: For still our ancient foe doth seek to work us woe; His craft and power are great, and, armed with cruel hate, on earth is not his equal.'"*

Nate slapped his chair. "'I've had enough of this religious malarkey,' Stockton said, scoffing at us. 'Let's go finish this!' Then, he and his henchmen began to walk toward us. Gabe and I braced for the onslaught, but before they men could wield their clubs on us, someone behind the gang in the cornfield began singing in a loud voice, and it startled everyone. The one voice turned to three, and three voices, to a dozen. Before long, a hundred voices sang out loudly the rest of Luther's great hymn of faith in God. I looked and saw people of the church, along with some others from the valley joining them, emerge from the cornfield and form a circle around the now frightened mob and Gabe and me. The elder I thought had deserted us was leading this large group and singing the loudest. While forming around us, they sang, *'Did we in our own strength confide, our striving would be losing; were not the right Man on our side, the Man of God's own choosing: dost ask who that may be? Christ Jesus, it is He; Lord Sabaoth, His Name, from age to age the same, and He must win the battle.'"*

They continued, *"'And though this world, with devils filled, should threaten to undo us, we will not fear, for God hath willed His truth to triumph through us: the Prince of Darkness grim, we tremble not for him; his rage we can endure, for lo, his doom is sure, one little word shall fell him. That word above all earthly powers, no thanks to them, abideth; the Spirit and the gifts are ours through Him Who with us sideth: Let goods and kindred go, this mortal life also; the body they may kill: God's truth abideth still, His kingdom is forever.'"*

"I will admit," Nate stated, with evident relief, "Never had this hymn been so clearly understood by me, and our congregation, than right then. We had sung it for years, for it was a Lutheran battle anthem, which spoke of standing strong against evil and oppression. It was at the heart of the Lutheran church. But, as time had passed, it had become just another song to sing, along with the staleness that had overtaken our spiritual lives. I could see the faces of the men and women around us, and I knew from what I saw they now understood the heart of this anthem. They also knew they were doing something which delighted Jesus. As Gabe had told me before that night began, there was more happening in the valley the last four years than any of us could have realized. The culmination of events leading to that night was designed to break a yoke of spiritual oppression and slavery on those people who were singing and demonstrating their support for Gabe and his family. It was about the people pulling their heads out of the sand and listening to what God was trying to tell them. They were now hearing Him, and they knew it. Three families had bound together to pray for the people of the valley, and we were seeing our prayers being answered before our very eyes. Spiritual and emotional freedom had come to them, and the insidious evil that had gained a toehold in this beautiful valley was being dispatched. But, the night was not yet over, for there was still much God would conquer."

143

Nelda took over, "When Katherine and I saw the loudly singing people emerge from the cornfield and surround the mob, we left the porch to join our men. We were weeping with relief and joy. I could see the remaining men of the mob had lost their courage, and were now cowering in fear thinking they would be treated as they had intended to treat Gabe and Nate. I believe if Gabe had not stepped in to protect them, they very well could have been beaten severely by our people, as some would have justified it."

I asked, "Are you telling me that Gabe protected the very people who were about to assault him and Pastor Nate?"

"That's right," Nelda answered. "Gabe spoke up when it looked like it was about to happen, and told our people there would be no violence tonight. He said it was up to God to deal with the men who came with evil in their hearts, not us. He also said there were some things we needed to do, and we should do our part, and let God do His. When Gabe spoke these words, a hush fell over the crowd."

Nelda continued, "Gabe walked over to the leader of the pack and tried to look him in the eyes, but Stockton just kept his eyes glued to the ground. The other men were scared and were looking for a place to run. But, the people surrounded them, cutting off all exits. Those of us who are still alive will never forget what Gabe said that night to Mr. Stockton. His powerful words spoke to our hearts as much as anything we had ever read about in the Bible."

"What did Gabe say?" I asked.

Nelda responded by repeating Gabe's dialogue with Mr. Stockton. "'Mr. Stockton,' Gabe spoke with a soft, assuring voice, 'Look me in the eyes. You will not be hurt tonight, so you do not have to fear.'"

Nelda elaborated, "Mr. Stockton was surprised by Gabe's demeanor and assurance, for I think he was mighty scared it would be payback time. But, he had no idea how Gabe thought, or what was in his heart, although he slowly began to understand by the way Gabe spoke to him. After Stockton settled down a bit, Gabe continued to talk to him in that soft voice. 'Mr. Stockton,' he asked, 'What would you do if you were me right now, and everything was reversed?'"

Nelda kept the monologue going, "'You know what I would do,' Stockton answered. 'I'd beat you within an inch of your life, and run you out of the valley.' Gabe listened to the response, but showed no anger. He paused, moved closer to the man, and said in a whispered, private voice, 'What makes you so angry, Mr. Stockton? What a price you have to pay to gain the things of the world, and give up your soul in the process! Have you not come to understand you cannot fill the hole up you have in your heart with more land and more things? The more you try to do so, the more dissatisfied you become, and the deeper the hole grows. Can you not see you have bought a lie the enemy of your soul has sold you, and, as a result, you have become are a greedy, selfish, lonely, old man? Can you not see what you are doing cannot satisfy the hole in your heart that you are longing to fill?'"

Pastor Nate spoke up to give his account, "We all were mesmerized by the way Gabe was speaking to Stockton. We stood very quietly, for we wanted to hear every word. It was as if no one was there except for Stockton and Gabe. It was a magical moment as the torches burned and cast their light on the drama unfolding before our eyes. We were unsure of what Gabe would do next. I watched Stockton, as his arrogant demeanor began to shift into humiliation, as he could barely look up from the ground. I'm sure the collective events of getting caught, being deserted by the men who came with him, and the outpouring of the people who came around Gabe, shook him to his core. With the last question Gabe asked of Stockton, I began to see his lower lip quiver, and I could tell Stockton understood things he hadn't before. I was also aware the Holy Spirit was moving so strongly that the scales of spiritual blindness were dropping off Stockton, and the other people who showed up that night. Then Stockton meekly asked Gabe, 'What else can I do to fill the hole up?'"

"'Mr. Stockton,' Gabe responded, 'He Who loves you beyond any person in the world is ready to give you the joy you have never been able to find, if only you will receive the relationship with Him He offers you.'"

I couldn't believe what I was hearing.

Nage continued, "Stockton answered, 'How could this Jesus, you speak of, love me? I have done so many bad things, if He only knew what they were, He could never love and accept me.' Gabe answered quickly, 'Oh, but you're wrong. He knows everything you've done, good and bad. He even knows your thoughts and your schemes that were never carried out. He still loves you, and wants you to give yourself to Him.'"

Nelda added, "We all heard Stockton whisper, 'How can this be?' Then Gabe stated so matter of factly, 'That is Who He is, Vernon.'"

Nate explained, "When Gabe used Stockton's first name, this in itself changed the way they communicated, as we saw a tenderness from Gabe that surprised Stockton, and all of us, for that matter. Gabe continued, 'Jesus gives us His grace. None of us measures up to what it requires to come into a relationship with Him. For this reason, He paid the price on His cross so you and I can be forgiven, and be able to come to Him. Our sins became His penalty to pay for us, and His perfection became our admission to His kingdom. It is not how good or bad we are, but whether or not we will take accept His complete pardon of our sins. His grace has granted us this pardon, if we will accept it. He will forgive you completely, and will be with you the rest of your life, if you will accept His gift of this relationship with Him. When He comes into us our lives, He begins a process that changes us into transformed men and women. He loves you into a changed life, and He will fill the emptiness you have never been able to fill by other things.'"

"At this point," Nelda added, "Stockton's lip was quivering, and then he began to weep silently as this information began to lodge in his heart. He was connecting with everything Gabe was saying. What really drove it home for him, was how Christ's forgiveness

146

was modeled by Gabe. After he composed himself, he asked, 'How can you forgive me, Gabe?'"

I was listening so intently that I felt I was right there on the scene.

Nate continued, "Gabe answered with a long, effective reply, 'If I truly understand the depth of Christ's love for me, and His complete forgiveness of all I have done against Him, how can I not forgive you, Vernon? I worship my King when I forgive those who have hurt me. You came to my farm intending to do evil against my family and me, but Jesus protected us. He deserves that I give you my forgiveness. He has turned evil into good, and you can share in His goodness, if you will take it. I forgive you, and I desire that you find in Christ what you are longing for to fill the emptiness eating you up inside. Look around you, Vernon. You see a work God has been doing in all our lives. Most everyone who lives in this valley is here, and we have come to understand Jesus must be Lord of our lives. We cannot allow jealousy and apathy to rule our lives if we want God to bless us. These people have come to understand for themselves that this change is needed. This is only a farm with a few buildings. God is not here tonight to merely save a farm. He is here tonight to show Himself faithful to His children who have sought Him, and to save a soul desperate for Him. You have it all by the world's standards, Vernon, but it is still not enough, for you are still alone and afraid. But, all this can change for you if you will allow Jesus to save you. God forbid that any unforgiveness on my part would ever stand in the way of you finding what you need in Jesus.'"

Nelda said, "With Gabe's last statement, we saw Stockton bend over and start to weep uncontrollably. Then he fell to his knees and began crying out, 'Lord, forgive me! Oh Lord, forgive me! I am a sinner, and I'm desperate! Lord Jesus, please come into my life and set me free from the yoke of evil controlling my life. Please, come into my heart and save me!'"

I was shocked, yet my heart was loving how the pieces had coming together, obviously by God's direction.

Nelda spoke up, "I watched Gabe kneel down next to Stockton and comfort him. When Gabe did this, Stockton wrapped his arms around him, while burying his face in his shoulder. They remained there for a long time while Nate and Gabe both ministered to Stockton. We could see the three men were oblivious to everyone around them. Someone in the crowd began to sing 'Amazing Grace,' and we all joined in, as Gabe and the enemy who came in darkness to hurt him, became a brother who was ushered into God's family."

Pastor Nate and Nelda's story continued to keep me spell-bound, as they shared additional details about what happened the rest of that night. Indeed, there was more to the story than Gabe and his farm simply providing food for the valley.

Nate pointed out, "After Vernon Stockton's conversion, more songs of praise and worship broke out. It was a revival like none of us had ever heard about or seen before. Neighbors began to reconcile with tears of joy. Feuds between families that had been continuing for several generations were finally ended. A spirit of oneness and healing fell over the crowd."

Nelda jumped in, "And as if to punctuate His approval, God released a much-needed element that had not fallen in the valley for over four years. It started with a sprinkle that soon turned into a welcomed downpour of rain! The people began to shout words of praise, and with uplifted faces and up-reaching arms into the rain, they offered heart-felt thankfulness for something they had taken for granted all their lives. God was speaking and the His people were finally listening. As a result, the valley's ecosystem was returned to its normal rainfall and predictable climate, and healing was brought to the land and its people. God's blessings on the valley were never taken for granted again."

Nelda finally finished the story, "The night of worship eventually ended, and everyone returned to their homes. Before doing so, Gabe's youngest daughter came running through the crowd and into Nate's arms. She exclaimed with a loud voice, 'Can we come out now, Pastor Nate?' Everyone heard the child's question, and began to snicker, for it was the first time anyone had heard their pastor, the reserved Reverend L. Nathan Schumacher, be called such a loving name. It was also the first time people of the valley began to call him affectionately, 'the beloved Pastor Nate.' From that night on, he was also recognized as the shepherd of the valley."

Yes, indeed! The story had more to it than just feeding everyone in the valley. I now understood how on one night the valley and its people had been saved from an evil force that was destroying them.

Nate went on to tell me that Vernon Stockton became a truly changed man, using his great wealth to feed and clothe the poor people he once loathed. He became a joyful man, and as Gabe had promised, and that hole in his heart was filled with the love of Christ. He never forgot the forgiveness given to him by God, as well as Gabe.

"Before that night, he was a man who would never forget a wrong against him," Nated added, "and he would always seek revenge. However, after his marvelous conversion that night, he cancelled all debts owed to him, which included those wrongs done to him by other people. Indeed, a true understanding of being forgiven moves us to forgive others, which is what Christ taught."

The story I heard from Nate and Nelda had happened so long ago that most of the people who gathered at Gabe's farm that amazing night have now died or moved away. Family members, who inherited farms, remained on them. However, *"When God returned the rains,"* is a story that has been passed forward for generations. It was not only a life-changing event, but also it was a vivid reminder to never allow spiritual apathy to gain a foothold in the valley again.

Pastor Nate and Nelda would die several years later. However, until they did, they became dear friends of my wife and mine.

Burt, at the general store, also passed, and his son now runs it. Maude Mae's restaurant is still serving its great breakfast, although

Maude no longer does the cooking. Also, there has been a turnover of most of the residents in the valley since we purchased Gabe's farm over twenty years ago.

But, the legacy of faith, and the steadfastness of the climate, remains the same. God healed the land, and it is still obvious!

CHAPTER FOURTEEN

The Secret of
Abiding in Christ

A s my dream of the past 20 years of events slowly fades, I begin to awaken from my afternoon nap against the boulder at my favorite place to overlook the valley. The sun has begun to cast long shadows across the valley as it moves down its westward path toward earth's horizon. Just before rising from my position, I hear children's voices in the parking area below my lookout. They are familiar to me, for I have heard those voices since their birth. They are my adopted grandchildren. No doubt, Ned, and his children came to drive me home.

Ned called from below with a loud voice, "You up there?" while looking in my direction.

"I'm here, Ned. On my way down," I answered.

Ned called back, "Pop, stay there. I'm coming up to help you down."

It didn't take long for Ned to stride up the path and join me. I guess all my family are concerned about my falling, and will offer a steady shoulder whenever possible. When Ned approached me, I couldn't help being amazed at the man he had become. With shades of gray in his thick hair, Ned was more handsome than ever. He has maintained his strength and physique, and he looks 10 years younger than his age. He's wearing clothes telling me he has just arrived from being out of town.

"Just get back?" I asked.

"Just rolled in. Mom said everyone has finally arrived at the farm, and it's time for you and me to start supper," Ned answered.

Ned and I have taken on the cooking responsibilities for "fried chicken night," when all the family gathers. Although Dottie does a fair job of cooking on Old Bessie, she would rather Ned and I do it. After all, it was Gabe who taught both of us what we know about cooking on a wood stove.

"You got Old Bessie stoked up?" I asked

"You betcha," Ned replied.

"Then we'd better go," I said as I began slowly moving down the path. While doing so, I took a last look at the valley below.

"Hold up a minute, Pop," Ned said, as he stopped me. "Let's spend a few more minutes here together. The kids are alright and are playing just fine down below."

I waited for Ned to speak what was on his mind. I could tell he was having a little trouble getting the words out.

"Pop, Mom told me the doctor said there was nothing they could do about your condition. I don't know if I like his answer. How do you feel about it?"

"Ned," I answered, after a pause, "I've had a great life, and I have a lot to look forward to what I'll have after it. If I only have a few more months, or even a couple of years, that is up to God, not the doctor. I feel fine, and I will keep running the race as long as I have breath. But, I will never complain to the Lord about not having more time, for He guided me with how to live my life without regret, and I feel satisfied with it. More than anything, I feel more close to Him now than ever before, and He assures me I have nothing to fear."

"But, Pop, what about those of us left who will not have you with us? I don't know if we can make it without you. I don't know if I can …," Ned whispered through a broken voice, and couldn't finish his sentence.

With Ned's emotions building, I wanted to say something quickly that would uplift his spirit. "Ned, all of you will do just fine. Your life is right in the center of God's will, and you are walking with Him. There is nothing more I can do for you that can compare with this. You know I have been very clear that my most important purpose has always been to get my family connected with Jesus, and all of you walk with Him. Ned, He will carry you for the rest of your life, just like He has me. I feel the same about Dottie and the girls, and their families. I have never been more satisfied with my life's purpose than where I am right now. I could step into God's Throne Room right this minute, and shout the most genuine praise I have ever lifted up because of the life He has given to me. So, let's live the rest of my days on this earth with joy, and not waste one day together with grief about what we will be losing. Ned, right now it seems to me I've been given a brief time to run a victory lap at the end of life's race, and to simply enjoy my final days with my family. God has given me the Crown of Life. I've kept the faith, and there is great delight ahead for me. Now, let's all enjoy my last days the best way possible, and look forward to when we are back together again."

I could tell what I said was helping Ned process his feelings about the situation. I know it will be hard for him, for I am as close to him as any dad could be. And, he will have his immediate and extended

153

family around him. It is the circle of life all families must face, when a child is born, and when he or she dies. The difference for me is I will be the main character in this drama, which is something I haven't faced before. I understand I must be strong for my family, for it will be my responsibility to lead them through this transition by the way I welcome death and God's eternal life He has freely given to me. It will be my most important time of encouragement for them as I prepare them for a life without me. Ned will have to take on a new role as the leader in our family, which I am confident he is ready for.

As far as I am concerned, I'm ready for the trip. For a while, I've been like most people in my current condition who look back over life and ask themselves if they have any regrets. Is there a damaged relationship that needs to be repaired? Have I invested my life wisely, or have I wasted it? When I face my King, will I be facing a stranger or a close friend? Will I be ashamed before Him, or will I see His delight when He welcomes me home?

I can truthfully say these questions have been answered by my daily walk with Jesus, rather than what I have done for Him. The Lord revealed to me a *Kingdom Secret* over 20 years ago that I consider being the most essential step I've ever taken in my Christian walk, which is to abide with Jesus. The abiding relationship I have experienced with Christ has brought me into *close proximity* with Him, and it is there He transformed my life. Before this I tried every method I knew, to try and change my life and become a "better Christian." But, the frustration I felt in not being able to change myself on my own, almost caused me to give up. Then I discovered the Kingdom Secret of *Abiding in Christ*, and God revealed to me it is in this close proximity with Him that He would help me become the man He wanted, and deep down the one I wanted to be, as well.

I could never do enough good works to deserve being welcomed by Jesus into Heaven. All Christians will enter His Holy Kingdom based on His grace alone. However, I do believe the *abiding* relationship with Him has enabled me to live a purposeful life, and the fruit that has been born from our relationship together will be there waiting for me. Jesus called it a "fruit that lasts." For several years now, God has taken from me the fear of dying and the sting of death.

I am assured the abiding relationship with Christ, has caused me to invest wisely the life He has entrusted to me. Therefore, I feel there will be a lot of celebration ahead for me. The Apostle Paul, right before he died, said he had run his race well, and finished strong, and the crown of life awaited him. I feel the same way, for I do not fear looking my God, my Savior, and my Friend in the face. I know He will welcome me then, as he welcomes me every day, to come and abide with Him. Therefore, I have nothing to fear. Would it be that all God's family could be so assured in their final days. They can be, but it will come from *abiding* with Christ.

As Ned and I make our way down the path to the parked car, I need the help he gives me to get down the hill. He tells me anytime I want to come back to the valley overlook he will drive me to it. I don't know how many times I will be able to do this in the future. But, I plan to take him up on it later in the month.

Driving down the mountain to the farm, we don't say much. The children are so excited about their cousins waiting for them at the farm, they are a bundle of energy. Therefore, meaningful conversation is impossible for Ned and me.

Driving into the entrance of the gravel driveway, I ask Ned to let me out of the car so I can walk the remaining distance to the farmhouse. As I get out of the car, he suggests he start cooking the evening meal for the night, and I can help out when I finish my walk. I agree, and he then drives the short distance to the farmhouse, and parks next to the gathering of cars that are in front of the house. The rest of our grandchildren run out of the house to meet Ned and his children, and the children all immediately begin some kind of game in the front yard.

I don't start walking to the house immediately. Instead, I just gaze at the farmland, the barn, the house, and the part of the road where my truck wreck occurred on that fateful, winter night many years ago. On that night, I walked this very gravel driveway to the house of a man who would teach me how to live life abundantly by *abiding* in Christ.

So much history has been lived in this place before and after that night. Dottie and I have now lived here the last 20 years, and have created our own story, and our own part of the valley's spiritual legacy. However, ours is a legacy built on the legacy of other people in the valley, as each person carried his or her baton for a particular leg of the race, and then passed it to another person.

Even though the farmhouse is a humble place, I feel it has been a refuge for many people whose life path has brought them here. What is it about this place? I think it is because the presence of the Lord is all around it. I think it is a place where lives have been transformed, and the Spirit of the Lord has the freedom to express His heart and values to people who enter this sacred ground. The Bible is clear what happens when God's people become "salt" and "light" to their world. Their witness is seen and felt by those around them. Quite simply, this is a place where people of the valley have had a daily walk with Christ, and the effects of it are seen and felt by the people who come in contact with its people.

As I reflect on this proposition, I ask myself, "Would that not also be true of a family, a church, a community, or even a nation, if we all *abided* in Christ? Would not the Body of Christ be such a powerful influence to the people around us, and the people of other nations who come in contact with our lives, that they would want what they see in the Church?"

I breathed out a prayer,

> *"Lord, this is what You mean by 'Salt' and 'Light,' isn't it? Your family becomes a seasoning to the world, and a lighthouse pointing to You?"*

As I continue my walk to the farmhouse, I hear a familiar voice speak to my heart:

"That is right, My child. It is as simple as what you have observed. But, it is also no less than this, for when My children abide with Me in their daily walk, a mystical attraction surrounds them. This attraction speaks to a hidden need lying deep within mankind. The influence of men and women who walk with Me, is caught by others in the best way. It is modeled by the way they live their lives. The people of this world are so beaten down, confused and disheartened by their lives that when they observe people who live above this conflict and confusion, they want to know why. For this reason, I do not exempt my children from problems non-believers have to endure. Because of this, I know there are people in My family who are confused, and do not understand why I do not remove their problems from them, since I have the ability to do so. But, if they would only realize it is because I want to use them for the redemption of others who do not know Me, that I leave them in a trial. It is in their trials and challenges, their witness is meaningful to the people of this world, and for this reason I help My children endure and conquer their fears in the midst of trials, rather than remove them from their trials."

As I listen to God speaking to my heart, the truth of what He says blends with my many personal experiences as a believer where I saw this dynamic lived out. I have been given a long, blessed life, and I am now close to the end of my mortal days. Although blessed beyond my expectations, and certainly what I deserved, this life has not been without the pain, tears and losses many other people have to face, whether or not they are Christians, or not. The difference is, I have come to trust God's purpose for my pain, and that He will not waste any of it, nor any of my tears. He has always had a purpose in mind, and His intentions toward me have always been good.

In most cases, I can look back and see how God turned bad things into good, and in some hidden way, brought a blessing back to me. Generally, it was only a matter of time before I would see this. But I had to learn to look through a *Divine Perspective* so I could see the hidden blessings for me. Losses that seemed unfair, or were brought on by no fault of my own, were overcome by God's ability and strategy to bless me in spite of the loss or pain. But, it would require that I entrust to Him my conflict and its outcome.

Always the case, my fears would be eventually overcome by trust in God's heart and promises. Little by little, I would be given an assurance He was with me wherever I would find myself, and His grace would be sufficient for anything I would face. This basic assurance, in turn, created an unusually strong fearlessness within me. However, this is not to be confused with a macho, man-made courage, but rather a calm assurance there is nothing to fear, for God is with me. This kind of confidence cannot be counterfeited, even though the world would try to produce it artificially in people.

The truth of counterfeit fearlessness is revealed when the ability to be in control of a situation is lost. It is then this false confidence crashes like a house of cards. The true fearlessness God provides a man thrives on being unable to control things, because God has no competition for our loyalty.

But to find this fearlessness, it requires releasing the illusion of being in control of one's own destiny to God, to find His peace in the face of adversity. It is at this point in a believer's life, true fearlessness is birthed and sustained, and it is an indescribable peace all men and women of this world long for. When it is observed in a believer by a non-Christian, it is a powerful witness, and can lead a person to the Source of our peace.

This witness is most powerful when it is expressed in the darkest and most challenging times a believer is going through. I can understand why God empowers us to sustain during a trial, rather than exempting us from the trial, for we are used to impact another person who needs Him.

I asked,

"What about my remaining days, Father? Will I still be able to serve You?"

The Lord answered,

"My child, do not concern yourself with this question. At any moment, child, I can place someone in your path who would be impacted by your witness, whether you know it or not. Just walk with Me until the end."

The Lord continued,

"My child, I am with you every step in this final leg of your journey. I will walk you into My kingdom, and into My presence, and you will simply pass from this life to the next as if you would walk into another room. You will be in a place you have deep down desired all of your life, and you will find a satisfaction you have never known in your life before. I have redeemed you for the life awaiting you in My presence, and from the consequences of your sins. Here, you will be given a life free from pain, sorrow, fear, death, and sin. You have no idea what it will be like to live in an environment absent of sin, and the brokenness that sin produces. This is a place your inner being desired all your days, and you are now not far from it."

I almost say, "Let's go, Lord," but I remember my days are in His hands, and His sovereign plan and timing are perfect. I am assured that I simply need to walk with Him in worship, and the rest will take care of itself.

I feel great comfort, as I walk the remaining way to the farmhouse. My grandchildren are running toward me, and the little ones will crash into my legs as they all race to their beloved granddaddy. I love every moment of it, and I cherish their laughter, and the love their parents give to them. I am assured God watches over these little ones, and they live in a home where Christ is Lord.

Oh sure, they will face the same challenges all parents and children face when growing up. But, their foundation is established, and I can entrust all of them to my King's care.

I am now close enough to the house to smell the aroma of fried chicken, cornbread and vegetables wafting through the screen doors from the kitchen. Smoke from Old Bessie rises gently above the roof of the house, and the aroma of oak burning in the old stove is an enjoyable scent. I hear laughter from my children and their spouses. Dottie's laughter is also clearly heard. It gives me great joy knowing they have each other, and to be assured that God will always be with them after I am gone.

As I mount the steps to the front porch like I did over 20 years ago for the first time, a flash of old Gabe opening the door comes to mind. His smiling face and loving welcome invited me not only into his warm home, but also a willing heart.

While thinking of this past experience, an involuntary smile comes across my face as I realize Gabe and his smile will be a face I will see when I am welcomed into God's kingdom. Now wouldn't that be something? To see that toothy smile again, and to feel the embrace of my old mentor, will be one of the best welcomes I could think of. Not to mention, I have a lot of friends and other loved ones waiting for me there, as well.

As I walk across the porch, a vision of my departed loved ones and friends come to mind. I see many familiar faces with smiles, laughter and tears, and watch them embrace me, as if I am viewing a scene in a movie. Suddenly, they are distracted from the attention they are giving me, as they turn away from me to look at another person approaching our group. The crowd parts in order to allow a path for the most important One of all to welcome me to His kingdom. He steps close to me, looks deeply in my eyes, and says: "Welcome My child. I've been looking forward to this day for a long time. Welcome to My Kingdom, and your new home. I've got a lot of things to show you, and I know you have many questions to ask of Me."

The comforting vision quickly passes, and I continue my reflection on life before I go into the house to be with my family.

I am at a point in life I had hoped it would be like, for I am living in a world with my loved ones, and with great joy. Best of all, it is well with their souls, and mine. I am also about to journey to a new life that has other loved ones waiting for me. I am a very blessed man, and I know it is God's desire that all His children find such peace, if they would accept it.

If I were to be asked how this happened for me, I would answer loudly, and clearly, this kind of life is the result of *abiding* in the Vine as Jesus called Himself. I would declare, if one would make it his daily purpose to walk with Christ in unhindered fellowship with Him, Jesus will create the best life for him that he could ever have, and it will lead to his heart's desires.

Abiding in Christ, and Him in you, will lead a man to the greatest treasure he will ever find. Remember this though; our journey with Christ will have many mountains and valleys, deserts and streams. Sometimes, you will be dry and thirsty, weary and tired. On other occasions, you will be living in luxuriant, green fields, with joyful experiences.

Life is full of both circumstances, and you will always have the challenge of these inconsistencies, for at any given moment, a good or bad situation can fall upon you. Even so, you will always have Jesus at your side. He will never leave you, for He will always guide you through the ups and downs of your journey, if you will learn to listen to Him, and obey Him. So, learn to listen to Him and follow His voice, and He will lead you to the place your heart longs for. I know this is true, for I have found this place, and it is so good. I cannot fully describe it. I can only say it is waiting for you, too.

Opening the screen door and walking into the front room, I see my greatest earthly treasures looking at me with smiles on their faces. I know what they are about to say, for it happens almost every time they welcome me when I enter the front door. Just like Gabe did when I would visit him, my family all says in unison: "Pop, did you

161

say hello to your old friend in Hotel Raccoon out there when you passed by his house?"

I guess I'll never live down that story, and it will probably stay in the valley for years to come. I'm sure Gabe is still laughing about it, even now. Who wouldn't? I still get a kick out of it myself. But, that's one legacy in the valley I wish people would forget.

CHAPTER FIFTEEN

Kingdom Secrets Summarized

The purpose of this chapter is to provide deeper explanations of the *Kingdom Secrets*, and passages supporting the thoughts. There are many more passages in the Bible that could be found, giving even more support. Therefore, it is recommended that these *Kingdom Secrets* be used to stimulate your own "Self Feeding," by finding scriptures that will be used to guide you in your daily walk with Christ.

The Secret of *Divine Orchestration*

Kingdom Secret: Life is not random. When a person abides with Christ, God includes this person in some way or fashion in His plan to reach someone else for a purpose only God clearly knows. In some mysterious way, our paths cross and we come to understand the encounter is a Divine strategy for a specific purpose that will touch another life, who will in turn, touch another life.

"Now an angel of the Lord said to Philip, 'Go south to the road-the desert road-that goes down from Jerusalem to Gaza.' So he started out, and on his way he met an Ethiopian eunuch, an important official in charge of all the treasury of Candace, queen of the Ethiopians" (Acts 8: 26, NIV).

"And we know that God causes all things to work together for good to those who love God, to those who are called according to His purpose" (Romans 8:28 NASB).

The Secret of *Divine Perspective*

Kingdom Secret: Our view should not be earthbound. A man who abides in Christ is constantly challenged by God to see things His way. In order to do this, we must abandon our rights to ourselves, and stop asking God to look at our world through our point of view. Rather, we should trust His wisdom and perspective, and look at our world through His point of view. Then, we are able to see through His Divine Perspective.

"And do not seek what you will eat and what you will drink, and do not keep worrying. For all these things the nations of the world eagerly seek; but your Father knows that you need these things. But seek His kingdom, and these things will be added to you" (Luke 12: 29-31, NASB).

"For My thoughts are not your thoughts, Nor are your ways My ways," declares the LORD" (Isaiah 55:8 NASB).

The Secret of *Divine Dispatchment*

Kingdom Secret: The right response to God's leadership will become natural, when it is God directing us, and not our self. When a man has abandoned his personal rights to himself to the King of Kings, he is then about his King's business. From this point on, the Lord will Divinely Dispatch us where and when He wills. Watch the way this unfolds, for it is part of our abiding relationship with Him, and the way He blesses others through our lives.

"Now I want you to know, brothers, that what has happened to me has really served to advance the gospel. As a result, it has become clear throughout the whole palace guard and to everyone else that I am in chains for Christ. Because of my chains, most of the brothers in the Lord have been encouraged to speak the word of God more courageously and fearlessly" (Philippians 1: 12-14, NIV).

The Secret of *Divine Preparation*

Kingdom Secret: God prepares the way for a person who walks with Christ. When God dispatches a willing servant for a Divine Purpose, He will go along with that person. We are never alone from Him, nor are we ever without His help. It is our simple work to obey and follow God, as we become His outreach to another person. It is a Divine Preparation of the Holy Spirit to prepare the way for us, by creating a receptive heart and conditions that will both introduce, and bring into completion, His purpose for us.

"Therefore go and make disciples of all nations, baptizing them in the name of the Father and of the Son and of the Holy Spirit, and teaching them to obey everything I have commanded you. And surely I am with you always, to the very end of the age" (Matthew 28:19-20, NIV).

The Secret of *Divine Dependency*

Kingdom Secret: Dependency on God is essential. There are two ways God's child can attempt to carry out a mission that has been entrusted to him or her. One way is an effort to accomplish a mission independent of God, using our own logic, talents and experience. In doing this, we will accomplish, at best, only what mankind can accomplish, which always has limited results. Then there's Divine Dependency. This method uses God's ability, His power and His wisdom. By accessing God's involvement in our plans, and take steps that come from His inspiration, we will see accomplished that which God alone can accomplish. He will do the impossible. But, in order to access God's empowerment in this way, we must surrender our prideful independence, and seek God's total involvement in our work. We seek His wisdom, and ask to follow Him, rather than asking Him to bless our plans, and watch us go. In humble dependency, we seek God, and follow His inspired plans. Then God is able to do His work through us, and enable us to be part of something bigger than we could do using only our own wisdom.

"You did not choose me, but I chose you and appointed you to go and bear fruit-fruit that will last. Then the Father will give you whatever you ask in my name" (John 15:16, NIV).

"Trust in the LORD with all your heart and lean not on your own understanding; in all your ways acknowledge him, and he will make your paths straight" (Proverbs 3:5-6, NIV).

The Secret of *Divine Interruption*

Kingdom Secret: In any coordinated endeavor orchestrated by the Lord, we are given only a small glimpse of His plan. Some people call this glimpse a "vision," and by others, a "revelation." Either way, rarely are step-by-step details for accomplishing this vision revealed. For this reason, God's child should understand that his or her plans, although inspired by God, might also be interrupted by God. Although this may challenge the order of our agenda, and sometimes confuse us, this does not indicate we are disobedient to the vision, only off track. A Divine Interruption is God at work, directing us back on path, so that the vision will be accomplished. Trust the vision, make your plans, but trust God's involvement, by understanding that interruptions are a way for God to re-direct our steps.

"In his heart a man plans his course, but the LORD determines his steps" (Proverbs 16:9, NIV).

"For the vision is yet for the appointed time; it hastens toward the goal and it will not fail. Though it tarries, wait for it; For it will certainly come, it will not delay" (Habakkuk 2:3, NASB).

The Secret of *God's Plan Above All Plans*

Kingdom Secret: God's Plan, not ours is always the right plan. At the core of God's Plan is our need for His involvement for it to succeed. This can be difficult for God's child, for it means that our only hope is for God to come through for His plan to work. But, if God has orchestrated the plan, and is directing it, then we do not have to prop it up by our own efforts. What better way can God receive His glory, and we not be misdirected by our own agenda, than to harmonize with God in such vital dependence? Learn how to listen to God and follow His wisdom. He will direct you to the right path, at the right time, and with the right resources, for accomplishing the task He's given you to fulfill.

"Listen, my son, and be wise, and keep your heart on the right path" (Proverbs 22:19, NIV).

The Secret of *God's Compelling Grace*

Kingdom Secret: There is a basic condition in mankind that needs to be re-connected with God. An empty, yearning condition in our soul exists, for it is created in our spiritual DNA to need an intimate connection with our Creator. This emptiness is filled only through the Compelling Grace of God, by way of Jesus Christ. When our emptiness is filled, we are then led to avail our life to God in such a way that the Holy Spirit may use us to effectively reach out to another person, and connect him or her with Christ. The ways we carry out this Sacred Responsibility may vary, based on the unique expression of His grace through us. But, the direction we point another person to must always be to Jesus Christ, through His Compelling Grace.

"But by the grace of God I am what I am, and his grace to me was not without effect. No, I worked harder than all of them-yet not I, but the grace of God that was with me" (1 Corinthians 15:10, NIV).

The Secret of *Right Standing with God*

Kingdom Secret: Christ is our Shield. There will be a time our faithfulness will be tested and rewarded by God's faithfulness to His promises. It will also likely be a frightening time for us. It is in this trial we are driven closer to God, or further away. It is our choice which path we take. If it is our choice is to remain firm in our trust and dependency upon our King and be pliable in His hands so that He can shape us, then we are in Right Standing with Him. The promise He has given to this man is clear, which is:

"The days of the blameless are known to the Lord, and their inheritance will endure forever. In times of disaster they will not

wither; in days of famine they will enjoy plenty" (Psalm 37: 18-19, NIV).

The Secret of *Saturation Prayer*

Kingdom Secret: The awesome power of prayer. In all spiritual confrontations with the world, the flesh or the devil, one of the greatest spiritual weapons for facing this great conflict is prayer. At the top of our prayer arsenal is Saturation Prayer, whereby consistent, ongoing, expectant prayer is given for the purpose of preparing for God's great work to be welcomed by the people. Never neglect this strategic use of prayer before launching into a great, spiritual battle.

"And pray in the Spirit on all occasions with all kinds of prayers and requests. With this in mind, be alert and always keep on praying for all the saints" (Ephesians 6:18, NIV).

The Secret that *Abandonment and Trust Forge Courage*

Kingdom Secret: We are "more than conquerors through Christ." There will come a time in the life of a true Believer that we must face our lonely valleys with only the fact of God's sovereignty and faithfulness to comfort, encourage and protect us. It is at this place that we must Abandon our rights to our self and to the logical and perceived reality of our situation, and then Trust God without reservation. When we face those valleys that challenge us using only one plan-God's Plan, which is hope in God's step-by-step involvement with us, we come to see those lonely valleys are places of great faith building, and we grows closer to our King as a result. It is in these valleys Courage is forged, and it is there that this man becomes more than a conqueror over trouble, hardship, persecution, famine, nakedness, danger or sword.

169

"Even though I walk through the valley of the shadow of death, I will fear no evil, for you are with me; your rod and your staff, they comfort me" (Psalm 23:4, NIV).

"No, in all these things we are more than conquerors through him who loved us" (Romans 8:37, NIV).

The Secret of *Divine Illumination*

Kingdom Secret: Light overcomes darkness. In the physical world, we know light dispels darkness, as evidenced by a light being turned on in a dark room. In the spiritual realm the same principle applies, as God's light will expose the darkness of evil. There will come a time in the life of God's Champion, when he or she will face an evil that will be conquered only one way. We must rely on God's defense, and His Divine Illumination to expose the deeds of darkness. Therefore, stand firm, and patiently trust the King of Kings to eventually bring His light onto the situation.

"Commit your way to the LORD; trust in him and he will do this: He will make your righteousness shine like the dawn, the justice of your cause like the noonday sun" (Psalm 37: 5-6, NIV).

"Your word is a lamp to my feet and a light for my path" (Psalm 119:105, NIV).

The Secret of *Abiding in Christ*

Kingdom Secret: The kingdom's greatest secret for living a faithful, abundant Christian life is found in Abiding in Christ. There will be found no clearer or more important instruction for right living and fruitful service than this guidance Jesus gave to His disciples in the past, and He gives to us now. When we live in an abiding union with Christ, we will have a life that will live with purpose, will finish its race strong, and will gain the crown of life promised to us.

"I am the vine, you are the branches; he who abides in Me, and I in him, he bears much fruit; for apart from Me you can do nothing" (John 15:5, NASB).

EPILOGUE

In the book you have just read, *God's Compelling Grace* is mentioned as a *Kingdom Secret*. I believe it is noteworthy for you to understand that God's *Compelling Grace* to me eventually led me to write this book, as well as my other literary works. It began with a mysterious invitation to come and abide with Christ. Responding to this *divinely compelling* invitation redefined everything about my life, for God's invitation is a life-changing encounter. But, He also offers this invitation to everyone in His family. If you will listen closely, after searching God's Holy Word, you will also hear His *compelling* message spoken to you, the same message I've been hearing: *"Come near My child."*

After many years of going through the motions of trying to live the Christian life, I finally listened to this special message from God. It was a breakthrough for me, for my hearing had been dulled because of many years of misunderstanding how to come closer to Him. Like many Christians, I was mistaken in thinking the only way to grow closer to God was by being busy with religious activity and doing things "good Christians" were supposed to do. When I came to understand it is by another way, God's better way, I was *compelled* to respond, for there was a longing deep within my soul that wanted to connect with Christ in a more authentic way. Even though I had attended church from childhood, studied the Bible, and had been involved in several different discipleship programs, I never realized this kind of relationship with the King of the Universe was possible. I thought, like many Christians, *"If it were possible, surely I would not be included in such an invitation, for the darkness years of my past would always keep me on the outside looking in. I am not good enough, nor will I ever be good enough, to come closer to God."*

But, I also heard another message in addition to His invitation to come near. I heard Him say, *"Come near My child by way of My grace."* With joy, I responded in obedience to this invitation, and His Compelling Grace produced in me a life-changing, driving force, to express outward what He was doing within my heart. It was then I also understood the privilege I had been granted to proceed on the path He had designed for all His children to draw close to Him, ... by way of His Grace.

Never, in my wildest imagination, would I have believed that my life could be so transformed, simply because I responded to God's invitation. It seemed as if a deep, unquenchable thirst within my inner being were being filled to the brim, and then overflowing. Then, I heard His message continue: *"Now bring others in My family to the Well of Living Water,"* and I discovered how God wanted to use me.

God's *Compelling Grace* is an open invitation that will ultimately lead us to finding what is desperately needed in our lives, and it will also show us how to effectively reach out to the people in our world around us. When we live in an abiding fellowship with Christ, He is then able to do amazing things through our lives. This abiding relationship causes us to express God's love to others in beautiful, distinct ways because of our unique experiences, diverse Spiritual Gifts, and individual points of view, born from our walk with Christ.

But, this unique expression must be enabled in order to be effective, and this is what God's *Compelling Grace* provides. We are enabled to harmonize with Christ, and as a result, we express "beautiful music" to our world around us. We also bring great delight to the Lover of our Souls.

Thank you for reading *Compelled by Grace*. I hope this book encouraged you. However, my greatest desire is that you not say, "What a great book I've read." Instead, my greatest desire is that you say, "I desire to take God's invitation, for He is *compelling* me to '*Come near.*'"

I strongly encourage you to take Him up on His invitation. I can testify that it has been the best invitation I have ever responded to.

— Rocky Fleming

www.INFLUENCERS.org